This book is due for return on or before the last date shown below.

5 DEC 2003	13 DEC 2010	31 OCT 2013
7 OCT 2005	1 MAR 2011	20 JUN 2014
17 OCT 2005	13 JUN 2011	26 JAN 2015
1 DEC 2005		28 JAN 2015
04 JAN 2006	15 NOV 2011	9 OCT 2019
14.7.06	27 JAN 2012	
19 OCT 2009	27 JAN 2012	
5 OCT 2010	22 MAR 2012	
22 NOV 2010	20 APR 2012	
6 DEC 2010	11 OCT 2012	
	18 JUN 2013	

Don Gresswell Ltd., London, N21   Cat. No. 1207   DG 02242/71

TONY CRAGG
SCULPTURE 1975-1990

TONY CRAGG
SCULPTURE 1975-1990

Exhibition organized by
Paul Schimmel, Guest Curator, and
Marilu Knode, Assistant Curator

Text by
Lucinda Barnes & Marilu Knode
Mark Francis
Thomas McEvilley
Pater Schjeldahl

Published by
Thames and Hudson
in association with
Newport Harbor Art Museum

Preceding pages:
Eroded Glass, **1986**
sandblasted glass,
25 parts
14 x 58 x 22 inches
(35.5 x 147 x 56 cm)
Collection Arthur and
Carol Goldberg, New York

First published in hardcover in 1991 by Thames and Hudson, London and New York.

Published by the Newport Harbor Art Museum for the exhibition *Tony Cragg: Sculpture 1975-1990*. Exhibition Tour: Newport Harbor Art Museum, October 14–December 30, 1990; The Corcoran Gallery of Art, Washington, D.C., February 1–March 31, 1991; Power Plant, Toronto, September 6–October 27, 1991; and the Contemporary Arts Museum, Houston, November 16, 1991–February 9, 1992.

This exhibition and its tour have been made possible by a generous gift from the Jay Chiat Foundation.

In Newport Beach, the exhibition and its accompanying education programs have been sponsored by the Orange Coast Daily Pilot/Page Group Publishing, Inc., the Festival of Britain, and the British Council.

The Museum gratefully acknowledges the assistance of the British Council in the organization of this exhibition.

Edited by Sue Henger
Designed by David Tanimoto

Library of Congress Catalog Card Number 90-71282.

Printed and bound in Japan.

FOREWORD

Tony Cragg's omnivorous interest in materials compels him to explore, reassess, and revisit aesthetic territory beyond the borders of art-world expectations in his pursuit of sculptural form. We are fortunate to have the opportunity to share Tony's work with the Museum audience in *Tony Cragg: Sculpture 1975-1990*. The exhibition offers a generous survey of Tony's diverse visual explorations, and all who view it are indebted to the artist for his challenging work.

The astute decision to bring a rich and representative body of Tony Cragg's sculpture to the United States and Canada was made by Paul Schimmel, whose curatorial sensibility has been a guiding light at Newport Harbor Art Museum and now enriches the Los Angeles Museum of Contemporary Art. Paul's continuation on the project was encouraged by Richard Koshalek, MOCA's director, who allowed him the time to follow through. Marilu Knode, assistant curator at NHAM, attended to the project details with fervent perseverance when Paul could not be in Newport.

Institutions participating in the exhibition tour offer audiences in other regions of the continent a unique opportunity to view Tony Cragg's work. Nearly all forty sculptures in the show will travel to Texas, Washington, D.C., and eastern Canada, thanks to Suzanne Delehanty, Director, and Marilyn Zeitlin, Curator, Contemporary Arts Museum, Houston; Terrie Sultan, Curator of Contemporary Art at the Corcoran Gallery of Art; and Alan MacKay, Director, and Louise Dompiere, Curator, at The Power Plant, Toronto, and their respective institutions.

Tony Cragg: Sculpture 1975-1990 would have been impossible to organize and transport without the generosity of its sponsors. A gift from the Jay Chiat Foundation has provided a generous portion of the support for the exhibition and its tour. In Newport Beach, the exhibition and accompanying education programs have been sponsored by the Orange Coast Daily Pilot/Page Group Publishing, Inc., the Festival of Britain, and The British Council. The assistance of The British Council in organizing this exhibition is gratefully acknowledged.

The success of an endeavor such as *Tony Cragg: Sculpture 1975-1990* is an indication of the steadfast support of the Newport Harbor Art Museum's Board of Trustees and many members. Their continuing dedication to an extraordinarily innovative exhibition program contributes far beyond the Museum's walls.

Thomas H. Nielsen
President, Board of Trustees

CONTENTS

Self-Portrait on Chair,
1980
found plastic fragments
approx. 92 inches high
(244 cm)
Collection Thomas Cohn,
Rio de Janeiro
Installed at
Lützowstrasse, Berlin

LENDERS TO THE EXHIBITION

Three Primary Coloured Objects, 1980
mixed media
Installed at Konrad Fischer Gallery, Düsseldorf

Arts Council Collection, The South Bank Centre, London

Angelo Baldassarre, Bari, Italy

Sergio Bertola, Genoa

Blake Byrne, Los Angeles

Tony Cragg, Wuppertal, West Germany

Galerie Crousel-Robelin Bama, Paris

Elaine and Werner Dannheisser, New York

Gerald S. Elliott, Chicago

Fond Régional d'Art Contemporain, Rhône-Alpes, Lyon

Marian Goodman Gallery, New York

Galerie Bernd Klüser, Munich

Kunstmuseum Luzern, Lucerne

Lisson Gallery, London

Anne and Martin Z. Margulies, Miami

Nagoya City Art Museum, Nagoya, Japan

James N. and Susan A. Phillips, Playa del Rey, California

Private Collection, Turin

Rubell Collection, New York

Galleria Antonio Tucci Russo, Turin

Saatchi Collection, London

Mr. and Mrs John Martin Shea, Newport Beach California

Mr. and Mrs. Ware Travelstead, New York

The Weltkunst Foundation, London

Donald Young, Chicago

ACKNOWLEDGMENTS

The exhibition *Tony Cragg: 1975-1990* is the product of countless hours working closely with the artist and examining an oeuvre that spans more than twenty years. First and foremost, we wish to thank Tony Cragg for the body of work from which a representative selection has been made. Not only is he lending from his own collection, but he has also made new sculpture especially for this tour. Tony has been most amenable in allowing us to explore his work in a reasoned and comprehensive manner, from his first mature work to the early plastic pieces and on through the castings of the eighties. His tenacious and generous assistance has helped define the comparisons necessary to create a revealing exhibition. What has made this project most rewarding has been getting to know the artist both personally and professionally. I have come to consider Tony as a close friend.

Also to be thanked are the assistants in Tony Cragg's office and studio. In particular, Peter Voss has handled the innumerable queries we have made regarding loans and our three-day raid on his carefully organized photo files.

We have been fortunate to have the active participation of Tony Cragg's dealers Marian Goodman of Marian Goodman Gallery, New York, and Nicholas Logsdail of Lisson Gallery, London, and their gallery directors, Jill Sussman-Walla and Elisabeth McCrae, respectively. They have assisted us in obtaining loans and have generously lent works to the exhibition. Marian, especially, was there from the beginning, bringing Tony and me together and working hand in hand with the artist to help realize this exhibition. Chantal Crousel of Galerie Crousel-Robelin Bama, Paris, and Bernd Klüser of Galerie Bernd Klüser, Munich, have been supportive of both the artist and the Museum by kindly lending works and providing valuable information.

Tony Cragg's sculptures range from fragile to immense, posing problems for their movement and shipment. In addition to the galleries mentioned above, I would like to thank the following individuals for sharing works from their collections: Angelo Baldassarre, Bari, Italy; Sergio Bertola, Genoa, Italy; Blake Byrne, Los Angeles; Elaine and Werner Dannheisser, New York; Gerald S. Elliott, Chicago; Donald G. Fisher, San Francisco; Anne and Martin Z. Margulies, Miami, and Kathryn Hinds, Curator, Margulies Collection; James N. and Susan A. Phillips, Playa del Rey, California;

Mera and Donald Rubell, New York; Charles Saatchi, Saatchi Collection, London; Mr. and Mrs. John Martin Shea, Newport Beach, California; Mr. and Mrs. Ware Travelstead, New York; and Donald Young, Chicago. We extend our gratitude as well to the institutions lending to the exhibition: The Arts Council of Great Britain, and Isobel Johnstone, Curator, Arts Council Collection; the Fond Régional d'Art Contemporain, Lyon; Kunstmuseum Luzern, and Martin Schwander, Director; Nagoya City Art Museum and the Mayor of Nagoya, Mr. Takeyoshi Nishio, as well as Takao Tani, Director, and Kazuo Yamawaki, Chief Curator, of the Museum; The Weltkunst Foundation, London, and Adrian Ward-Jackson.

The following individuals have also been very helpful in locating works and offering useful information for the exhibition and catalog: Christine Brachot of Galerie Isy Brachot, Brussels; Christian W. Kaltenbach of Galerie Buchmann, Basel; Valérie Chelle of Galerie Crousel-Robelin Bama, Paris; Priamo Lozada and Lydia Tzagoloff of Marian Goodman Gallery; Bonnie Rubenstein, Maxine Levy, and associates at Lisson Gallery; Jenny Williams, Curator of the Sattchi Collection; Rene Block and Yvonne Kennedy at The Biennale of Sydney, Australia; Susan Verschicelli and Marian Fitzgerald, assistants to Ware Travelstead; Antonio and Lisa Tucci Russo, Galleria Tucci Russo, Turin; and Barbara Mirecki at Donald Young Gallery, Chicago.

The Newport Harbor Art Museum staff has accomplished this exhibition under rather extraordinary circumstances, since two-thirds of the way through organizing the exhibition I left the Museum to become chief curator at the Museum of Contemporary Art, Los Angeles. MOCA's director, Richard Koshalek, generously allowed me the time to complete this project. At Newport Harbor Art Museum first I will thank former director Kevin E. Consey, who enthusiastically supported the show at its inception. Marilu Knode, Assistant Curator, has provided invaluable research for the exhibition and has followed through unremittingly with securing loans. She has been my partner throughout this project, and both Tony and I are fortunate that she agreed to take on the cocurator role for this exhibition on my departure. Lucinda Barnes, Associate Curator, has taken responsibility for circulating the show and has done an admirable job of securing an excellent group of venues. Lorraine Dukes, Exhibition Coordinator, has handled the flow of correspondence, travel arrangements, and other details. Betsy Severance, Registrar, has skillfully directed the complicated arrangements for the safe crating and transport of the works from Europe, Japan, Australia, and several locations in the United States. Also acknowledged and appreciated are Ellen Breitman, Director of Education, and Karin Schnell, Associate Director of Education, for educational programs and information; Margie Shackelford, Director of Development, and Kathleen Costello, Associate Director of Development, for obtaining funds to support the exhibition; Maxine Gaiber, Public Relations Officer, for developing the publicity program; Jane Piasecki, Associate Director, for the various administrative tasks involved in the show; and Sandy O'Mara, Graphic Designer, for related graphic design and materials. Brian Gray, Exhibition Designer, and Richard Tellinghuisen, Director of Operations, deserve applause for the design of the exhibition and for accomplishing the major task of installing the sculptures.

The exhibition catalog is the result of the dedicated professionalism of both Sue Henger, Museum Editor, and Peter Kosenko, Assistant Editor, who have assembled all the elements that make this publication the most comprehensive on Cragg to date. David Tanimoto, catalog designer, with Rose Ornelas, has created a handsome book that is respectful of the artist's work.

In addition, the Museum is pleased to have the participation of Thames and Hudson as copublisher of the hardcover edition of this publication. Both the London and New York offices have been instrumental in making the book available to a widespread audience.

I am very grateful to the participating writers who have been assigned the task of discussing stages in Cragg's oeuvre. Their essays were designed to help clarify the various impulses and ideas that recur throughout the works. I am grateful to Lucinda Barnes and Marilu Knode for setting the groundwork in their essay on Cragg's academic years. Mark Francis, Curator of Contemporary Art at the Carnegie Museum of Art, Pittsburgh, provides a view of Cragg's activity from 1977 through 1981, the year Francis organized the Cragg exhibition at the Whitechapel Art Gallery, London. Peter Schjeldahl, contributing editor to *Art in America*, covers the extremely productive and varied period from 1981 to 1986. And Thomas McEvilley, contributing editor to *Artforum*, focuses on the later works, from the mid-1980s to the present. All essays were commissioned especially for this exhibition. We appreciate the time and effort these writers have taken to contribute new considerations of Tony's work.

The opportunity to bring such an exhibition to this Museum would not have been possible without the imaginative thinking of the Museum's Program Committee, headed by Mrs. Charles Ullman, President. Finally, we are extremely fortunate that the Board of Trustees of the Newport Harbor Art Museum has the vision necessary to support original exhibitions of this scale and importance.

Paul Schimmel
Exhibition Curator

INTRODUCTION

PAUL SCHIMMEL

In the early stages of organizing the Tony Cragg exhibition, a museum director well known for having organized several one-person exhibitions around themes in an artist's oeuvre suggested that the secret to Tony's diverse and prodigious output might be unlocked by grouping the work according to subject and material. One would think that such a modernist approach to a body of work as encyclopedic and seemingly modernist as Cragg's would be viable.

Installation, Hayward Gallery, London, 1987

The most significant problem with this kind of approach to Tony Cragg is that it assumes that the work developed in a step-by-step, systematic, and signature direction, when in fact Cragg pursues his ideas in a far more fluid and amorphous manner. Thus, to organize Cragg's art by subject and material would be dry. What is so satisfying about the work is its generosity, its sensuality, and its ability to redefine the nature of the subjects that it depicts through the methods by which it depicts them.

Tony's work stems primarily from observation, from keen attention to the real world rather than from preconceptions. Instead of beginning with a program of ideas and choosing the subjects and materials to best represent them, Cragg consistently examines and responds to situations, objects, and materials from the world in which he lives. So many of his works begin with fragments of objects, both man-made and organic, purchased and discovered: *Bodicea* was prompted by a small bunch of plastic grapes, *Quarry* by a child's truck, and *Eye Bath* by a simple eye cup. The cast bottles and containers respond to their original sources, and even the earliest stacks and plastic compositions emphatically rely on the substance of their own making, the scraps from which they are constructed. Cragg is a realist sculptor whose macrocosmic sensibility allows him to reconstitute and transform objects in such a way that the viewer is imbued with his vision.

Lynne Cooke's reference to Leonardo da Vinci in her essay "Tony Cragg: Thinking Models"[1] has helped to confirm my instinct that, like the great Renaissance artist-scientist, Cragg bases his vision on the power of observation; a radical empiricist, he seems to feel that both science and art find their essence in man's attempt to decode the real. Da Vinci came to understand flight through holding a bird and drawing it. In his studio, Cragg can often be seen manipulating a small object in preparation for interpreting his observation of it in a sculpture up to one hundred times its scale.

The issue of whether Cragg is a modern or postmodern sculptor is moot. He certainly believes too much in both his subject and his material to be postmodernist, and he has none of the post-modernists' cynical irony. But neither is he a modernist. Seriality, or the kind of evolutionary development of a particular style that one associates with modernist artists, is not characteristic of Cragg's work. Rather, like da Vinci again, he dances back and forth between subjects and materials. At times his work takes on a comfortable baroque extravagance; at other times it is infused with a spare, lean rigor, a simple clarity. Cragg's virtuosity lies in his ability to swing between extremes of style, material and subject, and to recognize when this facility has gotten ahead of him, when the work has become too serial or signature.

Cragg's methods have little to do with either the art of our current era or with the tradition of twentieth-century art. Reluctant to be identified exclusively with "art," he juggles the traditions of craftsman, scientist, philosopher and entrepreneur, happiest with all his balls in the air. His studio is a factory of activity (reminiscent of Hollywood's depiction of Thomas Edison's lab in Milford, Connecticut) where six separate projects—aimed for Asia, Europe, and America—are underway simultaneously. What fuels his ability to keep up with these commitments is a pitch of creativity in which each project spins off some idea suggested by an earlier one. In his studio Cragg wanders from table to table and area to area showing his assistants precisely what to do, giving instructions about how to do it, and developing new sculptures. Many artists today who work with cast, carved, or constructed sculpture on the scale that Cragg does rely on commercial plants to fabricate their works. Cragg, on the other hand, creates his in his own factory, under his own supervision, with his own hands.

It makes little sense to Cragg to work on one sculpture at a time just to keep different pieces from vying with each other for his attention; he enjoys the dynamism of that free-for-all atmosphere, as is evident in the exhibition here. We have sought to present, in a balanced manner, Cragg's oeuvre from his first mature piece, the 1975 *Stack*, to a recently finished body of work made especially for the outdoor sites at the Museum. Although in 1987 the Hayward Gallery in London did an admirable job of exploring Cragg's major works of the period 1984-87, this first one-person survey in America is the most comprehensive of all of Cragg's individual exhibitions.

This exhibition and its accompanying catalog will be an index to understanding Cragg's single vision and multiplicity of interests. Instead of laying out the exhibition chronologically, we have elected to play materials, subjects, and years of creation off one other in an intuitive fashion. The catalog, however, reflects four significant periods in the artist's career, with the works presented chronologically.

Of the nearly forty works in the exhibition, more than half were made in the last five years. The catalog illustrates more than one hundred fifty works, showing in far greater depth than any exhibition could hope to do the nonlinear variations of Tony's prodigious oeuvre of over seven hundred works. It is fitting that, on one hand, an academic, scientific approach be taken to document and discuss Cragg's work while, on the other, an intuitive and poetic approach be taken in the exhibition, for Tony Cragg is an intriguing combination of poet and scientist, chemist and alchemist, believer and skeptic.

NOTES

1. Lynne Cooke, "Tony Cragg: Thinking Models," in the Hayward Gallery exhibition catalog *Tony Cragg* (London: Arts Council of Great Britain, 1987), 50.

TONY CRAGG: INTERACTION OF MATTER AND THOUGHT

THE INTERACTION OF MATTER AND THOUGHT

LUCINDA BARNES & MARILU KNODE

Tony Cragg came to making sculpture by way of science. In the late 1960s he attended a technical high school outside of London, after which he took a job in a biochemistry laboratory. Following his training and his

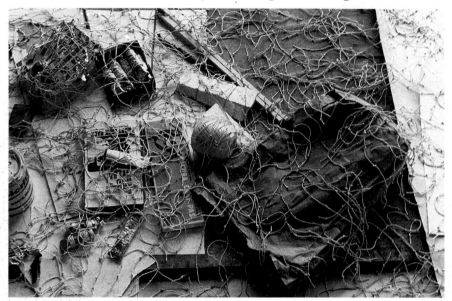

Untitled, 1970

Untitled, 1971

father's professional example, Cragg fully expected to go on in science and technology. At the lab Cragg assisted with investigations of changing physical and chemical properties. His work focused on minute, specific problems within large abstract issues. The long hours of laboratory testing, of watching and waiting, of relative inactivity, failed to keep his enthusiasm charged, especially at a time when the outside world was exploding politically and socially. Cragg simply needed more active involvement than "watching things tick and boil" could provide.[1] Though dissatisfied with scientific activity, or the lack thereof, the process of observing things, situations, and conditions germinate formed a crucial foundation in Cragg's art.

During the periods of inactivity Cragg began to make drawings, initially as a means to under-stand and visualize better the biochemical processes he was investigating at the lab. Drawing

allowed him a way to find images and meaning for things and concepts that really did not exist in physical form. In 1968 Cragg enrolled in a year-long course at Gloucester College of Art and Design, Cheltenham. The depth of his interest confirmed, the following year he entered the Wimbledon School of Art, where he continued to study for three years. At both schools the disciplines of painting and drawing were emphasized.

While at Wimbledon Cragg also worked in a foundry. Certainly the knowledge of casting processes he gained there played an important technical role in his later sculpture. However, one of the most immediately influential features of his work in the foundry was the labor itself. The physicality and arduousness of his job made it very difficult for him to return to his painting classes and work in a relatively passive physical manner. As a result, he began making things, but not in the traditional sense of sculptural objects. As a means to generate activity, Cragg began knotting strings. This grew into a productive process of making art that offered variability and a certain degree of discovery. It was the activity itself of making and changing physical properties within a creative context that initially fueled Cragg's early pieces.

The knotted string pieces became more and more complex. In a sense Cragg began to shape an environment, a culture of knots and strings. He formed a progressive linkage of material within which he could establish patterns and then infinitely alter and vary those patterns and relationships. The strings could be knotted in differing manners and densities. They could be individualized, grouped, regrouped, altered, and moved. He draped the strings over surfaces —a work table, a sofa—creating weblike nets of amorphous patterning.

Untitled, 1970

Untitled, 1972

man-made materials. Around 1970 he began collecting found things, from the streets or the beach, primarily human detritus, things washed up on shore or left behind on the ground—bags, plastic bits and pieces, and the like. Cragg started to separate and categorize his material data. In one series of works he separated quantities of found material into sealed plastic bags, establishing sequences of form and color. It was as if he were subjecting his materials to molecular tests, breaking down matter, or at least his material environment, into a system of particles that could be studied at close range. During this period Cragg preserved his work only in the form of photographic documentary evidence.

Cragg's works from this time focused most intently on variability, on permutations that could be seen through varied combinations of material form and activity. Clearly this type of investigation was stimulated by his background in science, though at first not on a conscious level. In the twentieth century the study of physical matter has been dominated by Einstein's theory of relativity and quantum theory. Einstein's theory essentially deals with the relative interaction of space and time. It suggests an enormous realm of matter and energy set in a state of progressive and continuous flux. On the other hand, quantum theory focuses on very small particle structure—atoms, molecules. Quantum physics promotes the notion of randomness, unpredictability. It deals with matter, not in defined or fixed positions but in a quantum state, one established by incremental units of energy. It is a theory of systems and the interference or interaction of units. [2]

In about 1971 Cragg exhibited work at a Wimbledon School of Art exhibition. One observer noted Cragg's shared sensibility with the Arte Povera movement that had been gaining force in Europe since the late 1960s. Until this point Cragg had experienced relatively limited contact with the mainstream of contemporary international art. His main influence was his immediate environment. Though he was interested in and encouraged by the notion of a shared phenomenon, from this point he consciously worked to avoid stylistic classification. That impulse continues in his work today.

Cragg's early artistic activities demonstrate a strong analogy with the theoretical foundations of quantum physics. While at Wimbledon he began to look further and further from the studio environment for materials. He used almost anything available, from food to discarded

Gradually the pieces left behind the sense of random scientific documentation and acquired a more poetic, personalized sensibility, a more focused and concentrated sense of activity. In the early 1970s Cragg made several works in which blocks of wood or stone climbed over the surface of furniture or crept up the wall. In a sense the supplanted matter had been removed from the logic of its everyday material function and implanted within an abnormal set of circumstances. The projects introduced an element of unpredictability, that is, unexpected relationships of matter.

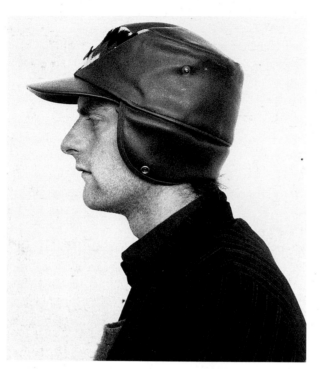

In 1971 Cragg also used his own body as an active ingredient in the work. In one piece he had himself photographed in profile wearing a winter hat. In the two side-by-side views the ear flaps of the hat were shown lowered and raised, documenting the two functional options of the hat. In another work Cragg was photographed outdoors demonstrating various arm signals, proposing himself as an indicator of directional forces as well as a human timepiece. The following year Cragg made a series of pieces using small round stones. In one a progression of stones meandered over an elliptical shape formed by Cragg's rounded arms and the upper portion of his back and shoulders. In another the fluctuating march of stones forms an arch from his head to foot. Cragg allowed the body to become the support structure or the base from which to examine permutations of form imposed by altered circumstances.

The human body softened the sense of didactic, controlled scientific experimentation and added a dimension of quirky humor and personality. In a work from 1973 Cragg was photographed outdoors, at considerable distance, supporting various geometric configurations of long strips of wood. His body took on an active structural function as well as created an animate, organic foil to the strictly ordered forms.

In another work from the Wimbledon period, Cragg was photographed standing on the beach. His figure cast a long shadow reaching toward the camera. At the shadow's side was its twin, the outline drawn in the sand. The shadow, and its shadow, dominated the figure as if replacing physical matter in form and significance. The work evokes a provocative sense of man's relationship to the forces of nature. Cragg's works involving his shadow can also be seen as homages to the life and work of Sir Isaac Newton, whom the artist admires greatly. In a recent biography it has been noted that "Newton observed the shadows in every room he frequented and, if asked, would look

Untitled, 1971

Untitled, 1973

at the shadow instead of the clock to give the time."[3] The beach work certainly acknowledges the late seventeenth-century physicist.

By 1973, when he entered the graduate sculpture department of the Royal College of Art, Cragg had evolved a series of aesthetic strategies through which he was able to discover and explore aspects of physical theory. He was able to integrate matter and thought within systems that marked human presence. His earlier scientific interests had transformed themselves into a materialist aesthetic, an attentiveness to the materials that inhabit our social and natural lives. As he noted later, "Increasingly, materialism embraces those activities which were once thought to be purely spiritual in substance and origin."[4]

When Cragg entered the Royal College of Art, British sculpture was dominated by a tradition established by Henry Moore and Barbara Hepworth, who based their pastoral, romantic works on natural biomorphic forms. Their impact was countered by the work of Anthony Caro, whose aggressive constructions using I beams and rivets introduced an industrial formalism decidedly influenced by the American David Smith. Also at this time, performance artists Gilbert and George employed their own bodies in photodocumentaries melding satire and intense personal and political involvement.

While at the Royal College, Cragg developed friendships with Richard Deacon and Bill Woodrow and came to know Richard Long. Deacon, like Cragg, was working with prefabricated materials (linoleum and sewn fabrics) and doing performances. Woodrow created recognizable "sculpture" by cutting images out of diverse materials. Long was known for his earth works using materials gathered on walks in the countryside. Cragg

participated with Long in several two-man walks between 1973 and 1975, reinforcing his sense of art as a physical activity.

Untitled, 1973

Untitled, 1974

Cragg often cycled to school on a tandem, collecting materials for his work along the way. In the process he rejected the more primitive, raw elements of his earlier work for urban detritus that he found by chance. This act of gathering depleted materials by chance was at odds with the prevailing linguistically based critiques of the art system as seen in minimalism and conceptualism. However, Cragg's aesthetic method allowed him to develop subtle analogies between human thought and its (often ignored) physical basis. The planet and its products functioned in the work as a grounding, one in which traces of human interaction with the material were never absent.

Cragg's works from 1973 to 1974 explored the effects of gravity and balance, entropy, and measured marking. In a 1973 work he grouped five brick columns of differing heights, leaning them precariously against the studio wall. Snaky trains of bricks twisting across the floor evoked the earlier string constructions. He also used wood in a collection of stools that

resembled a small shanty town; in circular wall and floor works supporting added planks; and in a skewed "x" of upright sticks. Cragg practiced a type of "deconstruction" with wood: he laid down various planks and sticks either separately or in groups, dissecting their natural grain with an "artificial" or geometrically abstracted series of diagonal cuts to suggest the way in which human manufacture stems from natural structure. He used materials nondescriptively even if he implied models of human construction.

Cragg came to see the limits of elevating poor materials and simple processes to art status. In Cragg's mind minimalism was actually based on a complex set of structures, and thus hardly "minimal." Much of this practice for him had become bogged down in mere gestures. He began "looking for models for visual equivalents of things that didn't exist" and sought to incorporate a scientific model of investigation (not mathematical but organic) in his sculpture-making. In the realm of science the notion of representation had shifted as dramatically as it had in the art world.[5] Much of the process-oriented art work of the sixties reflected Kant's phenomenological understanding of reality, one that eschewed the classical rational analysis and synthesis of representation.

In intertwining empirical perception of his physical and intellectual surroundings with a strict formal analysis of scientific and natural systems, Cragg imbued natural materials and forms with his desired meaning. He wanted to use scientific processes to better understand his materials and their aesthetic potentiality. Several questions suggest themselves to the viewer: How do themes arise from structures (material or unconscious), and manifest themselves in culture? Can artists use methodologies from the sciences to mirror the movements within society?

How can one effect a change from a dialectical mode of thinking to an evolutionary one? While allowing an open-ended dialogue for his works, Cragg nonetheless insistently searches out images and forms that do not have visual precedence.

Untitled, 1977

Untitled, 1974

In 1975 Cragg's activity-oriented probes of the random and potentially meaningful encounters between art and science produced a breakthrough. He gathered all the scraps of material in his studio, whether part of a preexisting work or not, and assembled them into two stacks, resembling configurations of geological strata. Embedded in the stack were egg cartons, building materials, and innumerably shaped and sized pieces of wood that functioned both as support and volume for the refuse sandwiched between them. Cragg's imaging of urban refuse as archaeological dig established an evocative metaphor of man's mark upon the earth and the interaction of natural and cultural forces.

Cragg continued to gather refuse, including bricks and concrete blocks from construction sites; but rather than simply pile these findings, he began to pulverize his data, dissolving the material that previously he had carefully preserved into a rainbow of colored fragments. The resulting surge of color restimulated Cragg's interest in the color theories of Sir Isaac Newton and Johann Wolfgang von Goethe. Cragg did not view Newton's theory of prismatic structure as completely opposed to Goethe's discussions of the emotions evoked by colors. His uniting of the perceptibly verifiable with unconscious, physiological response reconciles the division between science and the arts that has been well established since the Renaissance.

In 1976 Cragg completed his first descriptive and literal piece—*4 Plates*. Leaving one plate

intact, he smashed the remaining three into increasingly smaller shards, at the same time reconfiguring the fragments of each plate into a roughly circular shape reflecting its original form. Although he engaged an entropic process, Cragg maintained the appearance of the useful object, but in so doing he altered the object's literal and intellectual suggestions. With the lead into representation signaled by *4 Plates*, Cragg started to create more literally descriptive objects in a combination of manmade and natural materials. The following year, his last year at the Royal College, Cragg created an untitled work in which he cut paper into irregular geometric shapes and placed them across the surface of a table, a chair, and the surrounding floor as if they had been dropped in a vacuum. His 1977 graduate exhibition included a log-cut—a large tree trunk with horizontal cuts into which thin slices of wood are inserted, demonstrating the way in which lumber is dried. While he gave up the rather

Untitled, 1977

Stack, 1975
mixed media
78 3/4 x 78 3/4 x 78 3/4
inches
(200 x 200 x 200 cm)
Saatchi Collection,
London

theatrical performance aspects of his earlier
works, his new works continued to imply
direct human intervention but made the
theatrical space more one of interior thought
than of exterior action.

Cragg's work from this period increasingly
explored the tension between human structures
and hidden natural processes. He enlarged his
own understanding of the physical world and
sought to make sculpture a vehicle to expand
comprehension of that realm. Cragg was
interested in what Martin Heidegger termed
"radical astonishment," the search for the
essence or being of a thing. In the proccss of
revealing information, Cragg combined intellectual and material systems in order to shake out
new truths.[6] His works functioned both literally
and metaphorically, as material and fact and as
visual model for thought about the place and
status of their materials in our lives. Or as the
artist himself has said, "We find objects offering
up meanings and emotions relating to their
literal form, their metaphysics, their poetry, and
their emergence from the natural world, or
from their origins in nature."[7]

NOTES

1. Unless otherwise noted, all quotations of
   Tony Cragg are from an interview with the
   artist, 26 February 1990.

2. See Stephen W. Hawking, *A Brief History
   of Time* (Toronto; New York: Bantam
   Books, 1988).

3. Richard S. Westfall, cited in Catherine
   Lambert, "Tony Cragg," *Tony Cragg: XLIII
   Biennale di Venezia* (London: The British
   Council, 1988), 38.

4. Tony Cragg, cited in Lynne Cooke, "Tony
   Cragg: Darkling Light," *Parkett* no. 18
   (1988):98.

5. In discussing Michel Foucault's *The Order
   of Things*, Gary Gutting explains: "There is
   no longer any basis for assuming that the
   representative system of identities and differences yielded by, say, a logical or a
   mathematical analysis will express the sorts
   of connections that in fact constitute the
   concrete reality of things. For these connections will not in general be those of
   identities and differences but, as we have
   seen, those of structural and functional
   similarities. Accordingly, the analytic
   knowledge of the mathematical and logical
   sciences becomes sharply separated from
   the synthetic knowledge of empirical
   sciences." Gary Gutting, *Michel Foucault's
   Archaeology of Scientific Reason* (Cambridge:
   Cambridge University Press, 1989), 184.

6. See "The Origin of the Work of Art," in
   Martin Heidegger, *Basic Writings* (New
   York: Harper & Row, 1977).

7. Tony Cragg, "Tony Cragg," *Artforum* 26
   (March 1988):120.

Stack, 1976

mixed media

Untitled, 1976
brick and cement rubble

4 Plates (studio version),
1977
mixed media
312 x 78 inches
(800 x 200 cm)
Collection Herman Daled,
Brussels

**FULL CIRCLE:
TONY CRAGG'S
WORK 1977-81**

FULL CIRCLE:
TONY CRAGG'S WORK 1977-81

MARK FRANCIS

*New Stones—Newtons's
Stones*, 1979
found plastic fragments
4 x 143 x 95 inches
(10 x 366 x 244 cm)
Arts Council Collection,
South Bank Centre,
London

In 1977, before he had had a one-person exhibition anywhere, Tony Cragg was persuaded to exhibit in New York City. With the piece he made there (at the Fine Arts Building) he at once destroyed and recreated the tradition of sculpture in which he had been trained. Using a hammer, Cragg smashed a quantity of variously colored bricks into powdered rubble on the floor and thereby declared his independence and announced the level of ambition of his work. In this sense the crushed rubble piece seems to me to be much more significant and emblematic than *New Stones—Newton's Tones* (1979), which he showed two years later in his first one-person exhibition in London at the Lisson Gallery and which has generally been taken to mark the point at which his work developed a unique character. Within a couple of years, Cragg was to have museum exhibitions in England, France, and Germany, and by the end of 1981 he had developed an enormous creative and technical resourcefulness that has since shown little sign of abating. The years from 1977 through 1981, following the long gestation period while Cragg was still at art school and obstinately unwilling to show in public, may now be seen as a kind of professional, programmatic, and personal crucible in which he tested making work—both in the studio and on site in factories, museums, or galleries—in the real context of contemporary art.

Why was the crushed rubble piece of such critical importance to Cragg at that time and—in hindsight—to the development of sculptural practice in Britain and in the wider field of Europe and North America? It came at a time of reappraisal in Britain, when the radical advances made by the generation of artists who had left college in the later 1960s (Richard Long, Hamish Fulton, Barry Flanagan, Bruce McLean, Gilbert & George, Art & Language, and others) were becoming more firmly established, even

though the British art "establishment" continued to see their work as marginal. Typically then (as now) such artists had their first museum exhibitions in Bern or Eindhoven, followed rather later by their first large individual show in London or at the Venice Biennale. This generation of artists had been followed by what could crudely be characterized as the "Dutch Elm disease" school of British sculpture,[1] which banalized the conceptual landscape interventions of Long, Fulton, or Roger Ackling by an appeal to the supposed Romantic tradition of British landscape. This critical approach, if it can be so called, nationalized and localized the "new art"[2] and conveniently avoided the international links which were so marked a feature of the artists of that generation.

Against such a background, Cragg's crushed rubble piece seemed provocative. It was at once beautiful and violent, intensely colorful yet inert, industrial rather than natural. It ran against every precept of acceptable practice, just as it flouted every convention. One might take it to be the ultimate reduction to absurdity of the "direct carving" principles of Henry Moore, or the antithesis of the welded and painted steel constructions of Anthony Caro. In its form, its materiality, and its relationship to the ground, it might also be seen as an urban version of a floor work by Richard Long.

The distance between Cragg and Long might also be measured by a comparison between Long's photographic works of the period, in which his wood or stone sculpture punctuates an unpopulated landscape, and two photographs by Cragg, included in his first London exhibition, which show panoramic views of an excavated quarry in Wuppertal, where he was then living. These photos hint at the links between Cragg's work then and the work of Robert Smithson, Carl Andre, Lawrence Weiner, or

Cement Works I, 1978
photograph
15 1/4 x 49 inches
framed
(39.1 x 125.8 cm)
Lisson Gallery, London

Cement Works II, 1978
photograph
15 1/3 x 51 1/2 inches
framed
(39.3 x 132 cm)
Lisson Gallery, London

10 Green Bottles, 1979
glass

Ulrich Rückriem, who concerned themselves not merely with discreet or simple intervention with their materials, but also with geological, industrial, ecological, or entropic ideas. At this very early point in Cragg's career, we see the first signs of a much wider than national sense of terrain and of an inquiring attitude to material and site. By 1981 Cragg was able to articulate his interests in a statement, prepared for his first substantial museum catalog (for the Nouveau Musée, Lyon/Villeurbanne) but published only later in the catalog of *Documenta 7* in 1982:

> The need to know both objectively and subjectively more about the subtle fragile relationships between us, objects, images and essential natural processes and conditions is becoming critical. It is very important to have first-order experiences—seeing,

touching, smelling, hearing—with objects and images and to let that experience register.[3]

By 1978 Cragg had moved to Wuppertal, in the industrial Ruhr district of West Germany. He was working in a factory to earn money and had a small studio in which to make work and store materials. His intention was to develop his sculptural vocabulary of forms and materials in seclusion, without the pressure to exhibit in public. Nevertheless, he maintained contacts with artists in London such as Bill Woodrow, Richard Deacon, and Wolfgang Koethe, and with Jean-Luc Vilmouth, who had also been at the Royal College of Art. Vilmouth invited Cragg to exhibit in *JA-NA-PA* in Paris, where he showed his first piece made of plastic scraps arranged on the floor in the colors of the spectrum. The related piece *New Stones—Newton's Tones* (1979) was shown the following year at the Lisson Gallery—and the rest is history.

After the Lisson show, Cragg's long pent-up work burst out into public view in Germany, where he showed very large-scale "figurative" pieces in the summer of 1979: *Redskin* on the floor of a factory building on Lützowstrasse in

Flugzeug (Aeroplane),
1979
found plastic fragments
Galerie Bernd Klüser,
Munich
Installed at Künstlerhaus,
Hamburg

Installation at
Lützowstrasse, Berlin,
1979

Berlin; and *Flugzeug* (*Aeroplane*, 1981) on the floor at the Künstlerhaus in Hamburg, an artists' cooperative space. In pieces like these Cragg began to explore for the first time some of the metaphoric and imaginative dimensions of images beyond the formal and coloristic aspects of his earlier stacks and color-coded rectangles. The title *Redskin*, for example, refers both to the material and color of the piece's plastic fragments and to the form that had inspired the piece, a discarded tiny red toy Indian. And *Flugzeug* was both a template and a shadow: a trace and a portent of catastrophe, an enlargement (of the toy plane attached to a nearby

wall) and a reduction (from the scale of a real plane). It was as if Cragg's intense scrutiny of the individual fragments that he had been collecting from garbage dumps and skips suggested an infinite number of possibilities. (He also began to reflect, for instance, on the potential of plastic bottles, which later became such a fruitful and vital component of his sculpture.) These works, like those of some younger painters, dramatically reintroduced the problems of representation into the discourse of advanced art.

Cragg's work of this period was remarkable for its real human scale and its relationship to the visible world around us. It not only introduced representational images within the terms of strictly gravitational, floor-based pieces, but it flouted ideological convention by sticking not just the "model," but all the fragmentary elements of his sculptures to the walls of galleries and museums. The effect was startling. Just as the pieces on the floor were evanescent, sometimes almost invisible, and because seen at an angle, always potentially anamorphic, the wall works, although directly frontal and pic-torial, were hallucinatory in the intensity of their colored fragments against plain white walls. Cragg exploited these effects to the full. He showed a green leaf shape in Bristol, a blue moon in Paris, a yellow cowboy and a mountain landscape (from wooden flotsam) in Naples, flag forms in Genoa, and a lion in Venice. At times he was able to respond to the particular site or circumstances of an exhibition, collecting the necessary materials on the spot and making a work with some local or topical resonance. On other occasions he preferred to extend his explorations of certain personal concerns—the nature and function, or peculiar formal and an-thropomorphic diversity of plastic bottles, for instance, or the geological or archeological references of a stacked work.

Five Plastic Bottles, **1980**

15 Standing Bottles, **1980**

Redskin, **1979**
found plastic fragments
264 x 204 inches
(671 x 518 cm)
Collection Stedelijk Van
Abbemuseum, Eindhoven
Installed at Lützowstrasse,
Berlin

considered reflections on the use of the space, and by this point he was well accustomed to traveling light. Many of his works (with their folded paper templates) could be packed into a suitcase and reassembled on site. On this occasion Cragg played with the geographical and topical coordinates of the gallery, revealing with only six works a rather comprehensive overview of his current concerns. The Whitechapel's proximity to the Tower of London, containing the crown jewels, provided a pretext for the work *Crown Jewels* made from white (or dirty off-white) plastic shards, one of Cragg's most mordant and amusing pieces. On the opposite wall was *Britain Seen from the North*, a huge work in which the outline of Britain is turned on its side and scrutinized by a self-portrait positioned somewhere beyond the Shetlands, thus reversing the usual royal and governmental position that power radiates in concentric circles from the center of London. A political reading of the group of works was further reinforced by a gigantic blue plastic *Soldier* on the far end wall and the outline in wood of a *Polaris* submarine. Taken together with the *Postcard Union Jack*, these works captured a moment in recent British history when jingoistic nationalism, particularly pernicious in London's East End in the post-punk era of the late 1970s, was being fueled by the Royal Wedding of the heir apparent. The last piece in the exhibition, though, *Everybody's Friday Night*, gave the whole ensemble a modest, almost casual twist with its symbolic images of simple and harmless working-class pleasures—a pint of beer, cigarettes, television, and so on. Cragg's written statement of that year for the Nouveau Musée seems to acknowledge this modesty and humanity within the expanded field of operation he had set himself. Just when he was able to show widely (the following year not only in Europe but in India, Japan, and America) and to make significant large-scale

Another new point of reference at this time was a self-portrait image, always life-sized, taken from a template of the artist's body engaged in various activities. It became a curiously vulnerable figure, as if it were a late twentieth-century everyman. On occasion this motif is not identified in the title as the artist, as in *Torwart* (1981), shown in the large survey exhibition *Enciclopedia* in Modena, Italy, which represents a goalkeeper diving to his right to catch a "ball" that appears to be a rubbing from an antique Roman inscription. This piece fuses the vernacular with the traditional in an inimitable manner.

In the spring of 1981 Cragg was offered the opportunity to exhibit at rather short notice in the large upstairs space at the Whitechapel Art Gallery in London. He could have no long-

work, Cragg consciously returned to home base. He began to focus on

> simple processes . . . with materials nobody else wants. Ideas that interest me. Images that interest me. Made where people let me make them . . . . Works in which I learnt from the materials . . . . Meanings I intended. Meanings that surprised me.[4]

Without preconceptions and using the full range of processes at his disposal, Cragg worked in Lyon all that summer, at the invitation of the Nouveau Musée, on the "Factory Fantasies," which were shown informally in the space in which they were made. He cut an armoire into various shapes, stacked bottles on shelves,

painted a tree motif onto planks of salvaged wood. Later in the year, for an exhibition at Vacuum in Düsseldorf, Cragg reduced even further his physical transformation of material in a piece announced by a simple card reading: "The complete inventory of the objects in the apartment of Teresa and Rafael Jablonka. A work by Tony Cragg, September 1981."

Within this four-year period Cragg had turned full circle and was ready to strike out again with a new range of possibilities. In 1977 he had consciously built up a repertoire of techniques, materials, and concerns before emerging into the limelight of public exposure, distancing himself from his peers and working in some isolation. Since then a spectacular range of exhibition possibilities had presented itself and it is a measure of Cragg's deliberation that he did not exhaust himself in this outpouring of energy and travel. By 1981 it is clear that he was winding his work up to face new challenges by making a return to first principles and the simplicity of a pragmatic approach.

NOTES

1. In the late 1970s sculptors took advantage of the plentiful supplies of Elm wood that became available as a result of the Dutch Elm disease that decimated the English landscape.

2. "The New Art" was the title of an exhibition organized by Anne Seymour at the Hayward Gallery, London, in 1972.

3. The manuscript exists in the archives of the Nouveau Musée. See also Jean-Louis Maubant, *Découpage/Collage, à propos de Tony Cragg*, Cahiers du Cric, Limoges, 1982.

4. Nouveau Musée manuscript.

Untitled (Wine Bottles),
1981
Installed at Nouveau
Musée, Lyon

Tree I, **1981**
Installed at Nouveau
Musée, Lyon

Black and White Stack,
1980
mixed media
23 1/2 x 78 x 78 inches
(60 x 20 x 200 cm)
Collection Fond Régional
d'Art Contemporain,
Bourgogne, Dijon

Overleaf:
Redskin, 1979
found plastic fragments
264 x 204 inches
(671 x 518 cm)
Collection Stedelijk Van
Abbemuseum, Eindhoven
Installed at Lützowstrasse,
Berlin

Five Objects—Five Colors,
1980
mixed media
Green object: Collection
Musée National d'Art
Moderne, Centre Georges
Pompidou, Paris
Installed at Museum van
Hedendaagse Kunst,
Ghent, 1980

Boat, 1980
found colored wood
58 1/2 x 156 inches
(150 x 400 cm)
Collection Ida Gianelli,
Genoa

Bird, 1980
found colored wood
Installed at Lützowstrasse,
Berlin, 1980

8 Flags, 1980
found plastic fragments
39 x 23 1/2 inches each
(100 x 60 cm)
Collection Angelo
Baldassare, Bari, Italy

Self-Portrait with Sack,
1980
found plastic fragments,
canvas sack
67 x 25 3/4 x 15 2/3
inches
(172 x 66 x 40 cm)
Collection Sergio Bertola,
Genoa

Policeman, 1981
found plastic fragments
158 x 47 inches
(401 x 119 cm)
Courtesy Lisson Gallery,
London

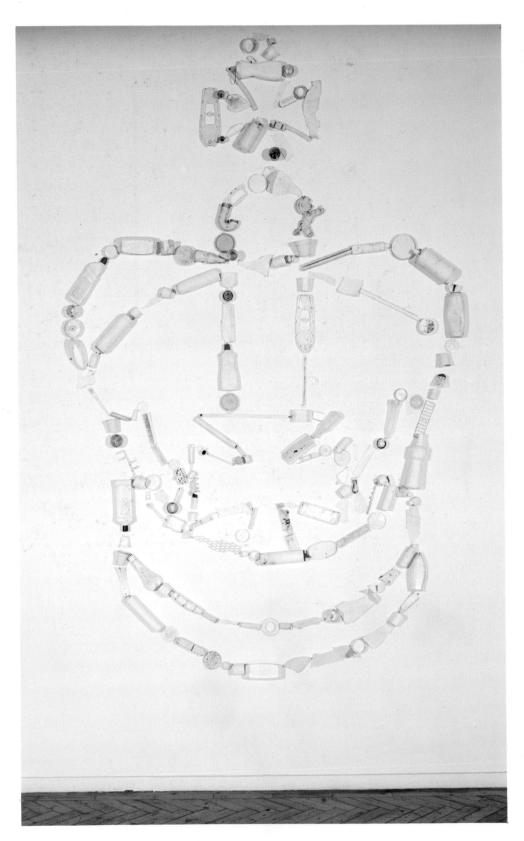

Crown Jewels, 1981
found plastic fragments

Postcard Union Jack,
1981
found plastic fragments
98 1/2 x 157 1/2 inches
(250 x 400 cm)
Collection Leeds City Art
Gallery, London

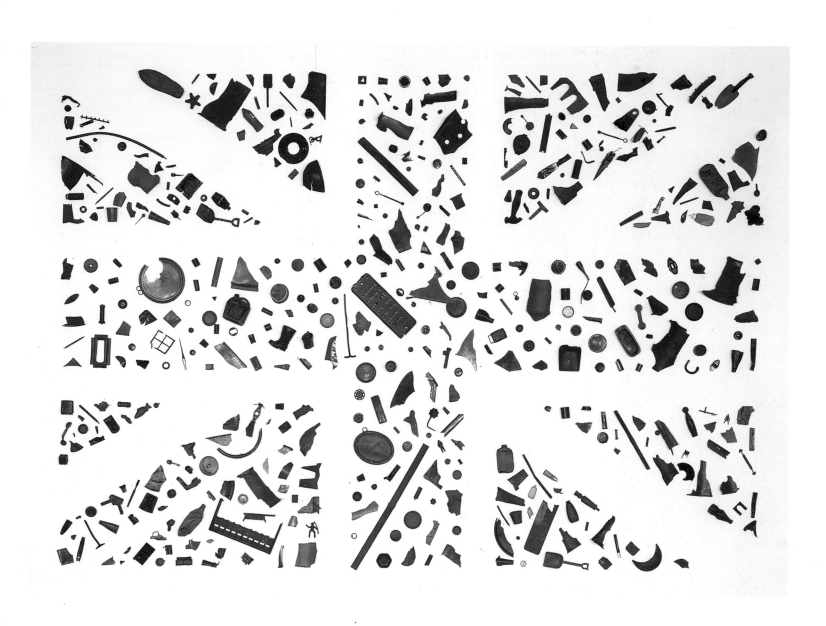

Britain Seen from the North, 1981
mixed media
figure: 66 1/3 x 22 2/3
inches
(170 x 58 cm)
Britain: 144 x 273 inches
(370 x 700 cm)
Collection Tate Gallery,
London
Installed at Whitechapel
Art Gallery, London,
1981

Everybody's Friday Night, 1981
cut-out found colored
wood
Private collection,
Belgium
Installed at Whitechapel
Art Gallery, 1981

Factory Fantasies I, 1981
cut-out wooden armoire
68 1/4 x 23 x 18 1/3
inches
(175 x 64 x 47 cm)
Collection Fond Régional
d'Art Contemporain
Rhône-Alpes, Lyon

Horn, 1981
mixed media
Collection Galerie Pierre
Huber, Geneva

Rockets, 1981
found colored wood
137 x 133 inches
(348 x 338 cm)
Courtesy Galerie Bernd
Klüser, Munich

CRAGG'S BIG BANG

CRAGG'S BIG BANG

PETER SCHJELDAHL

Five Bottles on a Shelf,
1982
plastic
13 x 23 x 5 1/2 inches
(33 x 58 x 14 cm)
Collection Donald Young,
Chicago

Like the swirling aftereffects of an old explosion, Tony Cragg's staggeringly numerous and diverse works of the early 1980s present and enduring, retroactive puzzle. What singular cause spawned all this? I remember the astonishing energy of Cragg's work at the time, in an art world drunk on painting and photography and largely inhospitable to sculpture. He was doing things with his plastic mosaics and with his floor pieces of found and invented forms that seemed incidental to the pictorial preoccupations of the day, and yet he was doing them with the magical authority of an artist possessed by the truth. What did he know that the rest of us didn't? His secret, I think now, was a long view or long rhythm of history, slowly advancing through his work even as he peppered the moment with rapid-fire inventions. Cragg now seems to me the central figure in a grand transition by which sculpture, long adrift in the wake of minimalism, drew power from successive, seemingly antagonistic waves of pictorial and semiotic ideas to reclaim its role as a pursuit fundamental to Western consciousness. The profusion of his work circa 1982-85 addressed a cultural crisis: a reign of radically uncentered, fragmented, heady sensibility, strong in the imagination that fuels picture-making (including the verbal sort rampant in the era's theoretical criticism) but utterly without any widely shared lexicon of the "body language" essential to sculpture. Taking the crisis head-on, Cragg turned it to creative account.

In the art culture of the early eighties, unprecedented infusions of private money and public avidity broke up the alternative-spaced, grant-funded, art-schoolish laboratory situation that pertained for most serious American and European young artists in the seventies. Cragg emerged from the laboratory having absorbed its postminimalist lessons of sculpture as the revelation of process and as site-specific installation ("stuff you wouldn't make unless you had a place to show it," in Bruce Nauman's mordant phrase) while shedding its pious tenets of reductivism and abstraction. All but alone among his sculptural peers, he managed a full-scale and undefensive response to art's newly frenetic estate: varieties of work ostensibly as theatrical, decorative, imagistic, and (more or less) saleable as the age demanded—the literally loopy figures of his *New Figuration* mural-mosaics were the very mirror of the moment—while profoundly loyal to a sense of sculpture's prerogative in history. The mysterious momentum that carried from one work to the next, in a hand-over-hand progress by which materials suggested images which suggested other materials, portended a thoroughgoing renovation of sculpture. By 1986, at a stage signaled by his turn to traditional casting in works like *Mortar and Pestle,* Cragg's aim was clarified by its conspicuous success.

Sculpture's prerogative is to confront us with the fact of our material, physical, bodily reality, making that fact available to thought and feeling—and making it sociable, an open secret shared with others in a common space. When it works, the confrontation is some admixture of seduction and violence. It is hard to manage with any conviction at the best of times, and the at once feverish and cynical early eighties had to seem a very bad time for the vulnerable communions on which effective sculpture depends. Cragg's aptitude for the task entailed a rare temperamental combination of gregarious showmanship and solitary integrity. His grounding in science may help to explain the tenacious discipline of his approach, and his expatriation to the industrial city of Wuppertal, West Germany, suggests an instinct for the off-centered haven that is also a promontory, a situation conducive to independent views. (In our time, individuality may be an odd mailing

address: think also of Anselm Kiefer in the Odin Forest and Bruce Nauman in New Mexico.) Not that Cragg's aptitude was readily recognized. Failing to grasp his art's long rhythm, many people at the time reacted only to its antic presentation.

Cragg's most common device then, his image-building use of discarded plastic items, lent itself to misunderstanding. Superficial viewers saw either a gross whimsicality, predicated on the assumption that plastic refuse is dreck beneath contempt, or the ecological good-boyism of an exemplary recycler. Such viewers suffered from the social bias that blocks raw edges of reality with off-the-shelf "values." (All of us are such viewers at least some of the time, subject to the groggy deliriums of an image-sickened, body-denying, atomized society numbed to the spirit both in things and in ourselves.) In truth, Cragg's aesthetic use of trashed plastic was a stratagem for catching naked reality by surprise, seizing on stuff whose "worthlessness" is precisely a condition of freedom *to be*, an ontological innocence. Modern art has been employing found objects for eight decades, of course—from Braque's bits of wallpaper to Richard Long's rocks—but generally subject to some artifying displacement by which either nature or culture, or both, imparts a poetic aura. (The Duchampian readymade is another matter, which I'll get to.) Cragg's innovation was to locate *and to maintain* his materials in the very teeth of socially determined meaning, the semiotic maelstrom of function and design, use and disposal. Each component of an early eighties Cragg is apt to bristle with information about the civilization that commanded its existence, meanwhile obediently combining (like iron filings in a magnetic field) in the template of a no less overdetermined image. The image, in turn, is introduced into the signifying social web of its

installation in a museum, a gallery, or a home. The image and the installation don't dilute the actuality of the components. They intensify it. Cragg sought the ideal of sculpture—a silence of sheerly beholding—not in types of distancing that fill found objects with nostalgia, but in the present-tense din of the manufactured world. Cragg's is a silence made of clamor, visible white noise—most emphatically in the mosaics, through which he explored sculpture's capacity for formal dynamics and a sociable content that were really new.

Afternoon light was soft in the collector's house on Long Island where recently I sat down with my notebook, feeling like an interrogator, to watch a mosaic titled *Blue Indian* (1983). One does *watch* rather than *look at* Cragg's mosaics, I've decided. Looking-at is reserved for the work's constituent parts, its units and fragments of poignant detritus. *Taking in* seems the right phrase for registration of the work's overall shape, which in this instance was the head-on silhouette of an American Indian leaping forward with a rifle (modeled on a tiny plastic toy figurine glued alongside as an apostrophe, certifying the image as a cultural datum). Between the active looking-at, in detail, and the passive taking-in, in toto, you engage in watchfulness that might also be termed *attendance* (waiting with, waiting on). I was aware of time flowing in the room. I sat with the mosaic in silence as you would with a friend who is thinking something over. I noted the work's plenitude, its teeming liveliness of address like a miracle of generosity in the unscheduled afternoon. I noted its color. "Slate to dusty blue-green to true blue to cobalt," I scribbled. The mosaic is all blues, selected from the universe of discarded plastic stuff by that chromatic criterion, and I felt guilty that I had never done justice, by carefully noticing, the wonders of blue. Here was a chance of atonement.

Three Forks, 1982
white paint on found
colored wood

Dining Motions, 1982
white paint on found
colored wood
127 x 295 inches
(323 x 749 cm)
Donald Young Gallery,
Chicago

"Is Cragg mosaic 'relief'?" I wrote. "No." Relief works as a meaningful distortion, an extrusion, of the wall, which "comes to life." A Cragg mosaic, being open, allows the wall to pass through it undisturbed, like light through unrefracting glass. (My eye reads the mosaic *within* the wall plane rather than in front of it, an effect no less persuasive for insulting common sense. But then, do we ever look *at* a wall? A wall may be less a thing seen than a condition of seeing.) The wall is a passive though energized field for the location of each constituent part of the mosaic. The mosaic's active, taken-in field is strictly mental: the viewer's recognition of "an Indian." The objective plastic items and the subjective image oscillate like a reversible figure-ground relation, starting a pulse in consciousness: that afternoon, the ghostly Indian alternately leaping out at me bodily and disintegrating back into a welter of impertinent specificities. The pulse governs in time—the time of watching—a meditation on social references (for instance, the awful processes by which the American Indian was

romantically imagined and, simultaneously, destroyed) and the agreeable shock of poetic sensation (for instance, terror and tenderness of blue). You cannot exhaust the dynamic, only yourself. After twenty minutes I was tired out by *Blue Indian*—pleasantly so, as after a swim—and looked away.

Tony Cragg in the early eighties showed that sculpture could occupy the wall and even "make a picture" without succumbing to pictorial aesthetics. The key was loyalty to the absolute authority—compound of seduction and violence, commanding love and fear—of *matter*. Cragg tested that authority with his audaciously conceived picture-like uses for sculpture—optical (with color), compositional (with rhythmic weights), representational (with loaded images)—but with a deep intent to praise matter, not bury it. "I am an extreme materialist," he has said, by which he seems to mean an anti-idealism pushed so far that it begins to connect, ecstatically, with its opposite. His uses of plastic refuse suggest that a sacredness of *what is* may inhere most keenly in despised things. "I want objects to stand there just like they should be there, like they have actually earned their place," Cragg said in a 1986 interview with Lynne Cooke, gently stating something momentous. "They're there and they want a dialogue on the basis of all the other things in the world, and not on the basis of a particular group of objects which one has called, in the past, 'sculpture.'" Observe that this is not the same as saying, as we do of Duchampian readymades, that any object can be made "sculpture" by a shift in context. The readymade is only too happy to welcome and preserve our contempt for, say, a urinal, the better to ironize "art." Cragg is never ironic, always in earnest. (Even his abundant wit is earnest, as in such politically edged pieces of the early eighties as a Mercedes-Benz symbol

made of riot-stuff: bricks and bottles.) Cragg calls on "sculpture" to admit its fraternity in the republic of existence, where no object is a second-class citizen.

Axehead, 1982
wood and mixed media,
48 parts
45 x 154 3/4 x 193
inches
(109 x 393 x 490 cm)
Collection Tate Gallery,
London

Oval, 1982
mixed media
119 x 91 2/3 x 17 inches
(290 x 235 x 43 cm)
Dart Gallery, Inc.,
Chicago, Illinois

Think of a spent plastic cigarette lighter in a junkyard, lying on the ground—an intimately human-complicit object (the appurtenance of a human addiction) as permanent as a stone. Pick it up. It is good for nothing now, though the story of its function surrounds it like a haze. Cut through the haze. Can you begin simply to behold the thing? But it's not so simple. Your mind is working in its relentless way, tugging you up from naked vision into your mental library of categories and associations. Words rehaze the cigarette lighter. "Artificial," for instance. As opposed to "natural." Can you feel the violence being done to the reality of what you hold by that reflexive distinction, with its moralizing undertones? Seek help from scientific knowledge. What is the lighter, in fact, made of? Petrochemicals, remnants of ancient life. The chemicals were cooked together by humans rather than spewed from a volcano, say, but are humans "artificial"? Are you? Cragg has commented on a capital example of such semantic tyranny: we call the nest a bird builds "natural," but the house a human builds

"artificial." I think, too, of something an American Indian is supposed to have told a visitor who marveled at his tribe's ability to keep old cars running indefinitely: "You white men think everything is dead." Use the crystalline impartiality of scientific description to disperse the verbal haze blocking both your vision and your knowledge of the lighter. You are now ready for a go at Tony Cragg, in whose works each object sings its being.

If I am making Tony Cragg sound like a Walt Whitman of the inanimate, good. I don't think that's a far-fetched analogy, since the artist's dominant emotional tone seems quite close to what Whitman meant by the virtue of "adhesiveness": an erotic predilection for the world. Perusing the components of a work by Cragg can make me feel like St. Francis hailing birds one by one, greeting each bright, small, concentrated existence with funny tenderness. It can also feel like serious flirting. The feeling is active, even strenuous, and requires attention that is constantly renewed by acts of will. Viewing a show of Cragg's work is like climbing a steep hill to discover another hill, and another. Your reward for the exertion is a visceral sense of the artist's appetite for the real, and of your own—strength meeting strength as in a friendly wrestling match with mutual exaltation (until you are exhausted). Cragg's reward is a fantastic range of freedom in material and form, a liberty to make any sort of object at all—even "sculpture."

The freedom Cragg had earned by 1984-85 is apparent in the distinctive particularities of *Three Modern Buildings*, *Silent Place with Dwelling*, and *Echo*. All these works may be termed "discursive," in my dictionary's sense of "proceeding by reasoning or argument rather than intuition." Not that the "reasoning or argument" is ever clear, and not that the

sculptures aren't, in humble point of truth, products of one intuition after another. I'm talking about the character of the viewer's engagement with the work. The work's structural tone is indeed one of deliberate "proceeding": things and qualities proceeding from, with, and against each other with methodical logic no less sweetly reasonable for being obscure. The logic is embedded in the physical and suggestive nature of the materials, expressing not the artist's meaning—so one feels, as one gazes—but their own. In *Three Modern Buildings*, bricks and cinder blocks fulfill their congenital destiny of making architecture. Never mind that the architecture is useless to humans. Human use is a concept beyond the intellectual capacity of cinder blocks, which are doing the best they can with what they know. They know their own strength and beauty and how to work together—nothing if not team players, are cinder blocks—to become something even stronger and more beautiful. Confronting these works, I envy the fun of being a cinder block.

The discourse of *Silent Place with Dwelling*, a notably lovely piece, feels narrative. Not that it "tells a story." Rather, it *is* a story, told in chunks of wood that, like paragraphs or stanzas, say to me (reading from top to bottom) "sky" (or maybe "moonrise"), "house seen in passing" (suggestion of its cubistic distortion), "earth," and "altitude." The loveliness of the work's title is in its redundancy, telling us something we know already just from looking: the sculpture says "silent place with dwelling" more powerfully than words can, such that the words add a pleasant surfeit—an overflow—of meaning. No longer, as in his mosaics, is Cragg submitting materials to the marching orders of preexisting images. Here I feel it is a memory or dream that has caused the wood chunks to arrange themselves, all but quivering with enchantment as they try in their awkward way to get the thing right.

Cragg has said that *Echo* was indeed inspired by a memory of driving from Lille to Turin over Mont Blanc. Would we recognize aspects of the sculpture along that route if we drove it? Probably not, and it doesn't matter. We recognize in the sculpture the character of any passing scene, things simultaneously standing out in their peculiarity and relating—relations continuously unfolding, shifting, and collapsing—to the peculiarity of other things. What of Cragg's allover scribbling on *Echo*'s surfaces? I think it functions as a map of sight, a tracery of eye-movements that feel out and constellate, in the mind, a seen thing's solidity. The complexity of Cragg's aesthetic dialectic, and the range of options it gives him, is amazing. It can draw us bodily to the body of the sculpture, as in the infectiously foursquare *Three Modern Buildings*, or it can disembody the sculpture and deliver it—as something predigested, preseen—into our minds, as with *Echo*. Something of both dynamics occurs in *Mortar and Pestle* of 1986, where the process of casting contributes its own discursive overtone, telling us that there actually exists or has existed, in another material, forms of exactly these two objects—in the same preposterous sizes. The sensual forms dimly recall a pharmacist's implements and vividly contemplate sex.

Not to poach on the next essayist's territory, I stop here with my sketch of the "extreme materialist" dialectics that in Cragg's work since 1985 has exfoliated so many presences. I've tried to show the growth of a sculptural idea: an idea *of* sculpture *in* sculpture, by which Cragg in the early eighties put his art in touch with its old prerogative and built it a repertoire of new means for engaging and moving the world. I have left out, lacking space to do it justice, the fascinating theme of Cragg's influence in art of the eighties, an influence most directly apparent in the decade's

Palette, 1982

white paint on found
colored boards

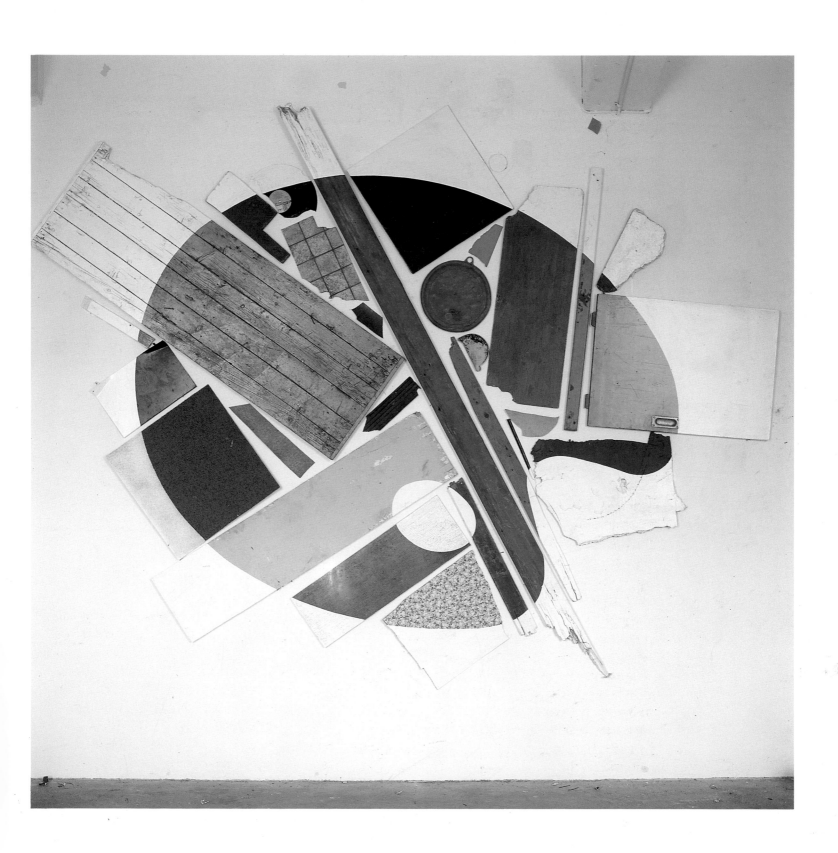

estimable contingent of new British sculptors but extending in subtle ways, which careful criticism might tease out, even to artists who are temperamentally his antagonists. Is Cragg's wonderful *Five Bottles on a Shelf* of 1982 at the root of neo-geo? Certainly no other artist since Andy Warhol has done more to expose the wildly yearning soul of manufactured goods—and Cragg did it, in the early eighties, almost as an aside, incidental to the larger game he was pursuing. This, too, is a still tumbling effect of the explosion—Cragg's big bang—without which, art of the last ten years would surely be markedly different and poorer.

Chair, 1982
mixed media on metal
frame
Installed near Chambéry,
France

Two Positions, 1983
wood furniture, stone
37 1/2 x 62 1/2 x 62 1/2
inches
(95 x 159 x 159 cm)
Collection Anne and
Martin Z. Margulies,
Miami

Installation at Konrad Fischer Gallery, Düsseldorf, 1982-83:

House, 1982
mixed media on metal frame
62 1/2 x 66 1/3 x 39 inches
(160 x 170 x 100 cm)
Konrad Fischer Gallery, Düsseldorf

Trough, 1982
mixed media
35 x 97 1/2 x 35 inches
(90 x 250 x 90 cm)
Konrad Fischer Gallery, Düsseldorf

Mercedes, 1982
bricks and bottles
117 inches diameter (300 cm)
Collection Sylvia Pearlstein, Antwerp, courtesy Galerie Christine and Isy Brachot, Brussels

Large Window III, 1983
white paint on found colored wood
106 x 80 inches
(269 x 203 cm)
Collection James N. and Susan A. Phillips, Playa del Rey, California

Some Kind of a Group,
1983
, mixed media
75 1/2 x 360 inches
(192 x 914 cm)
Collection U.S. Trust

Leaf, 1982
found plastic fragments

Landscape on Wall, 1983
found colored wood

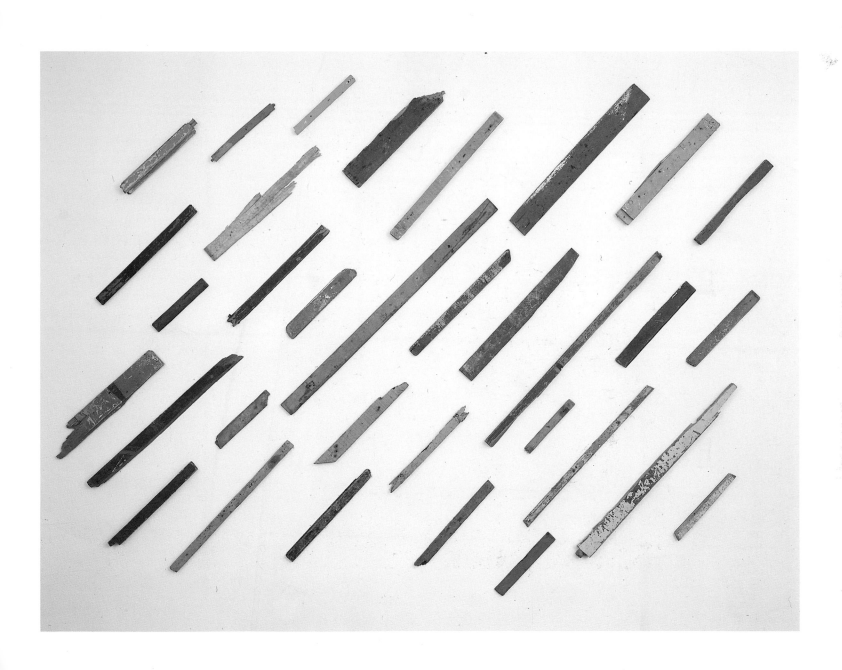

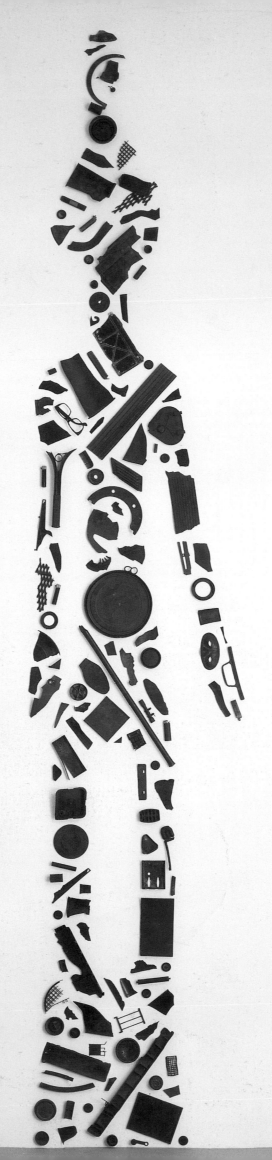

African Culture Myth,
1984
found plastic fragments
164 x 39 inches
(420 x 100 cm)
Collection Kunstmuseum
Luzern, Lucerne

Installation at Kunsthalle
Waaghaus, Winterthur,
1985:
African Culture Myth,
1984
Spectrum, 1983
found plastic fragments
253 x 136 inches
(650 x 350 cm)
Private collection,
Germany

Houses in Fjord, 1985
stone
Installed near Oslo,
Norway, 1985

Silent Place with Dwelling,
1984
wood
60 1/2 x 41 x 23 1/2
inches
(155 x 105 x 60 cm)
Collection Nagoya City
Art Museum, Nagoya,
Japan

Mittelschicht, 1984
wood
59 x 156 x 156 inches
(152 x 400 x 650 cm)
Private collection,
courtesy Galleria Tucci
Russo, Turin

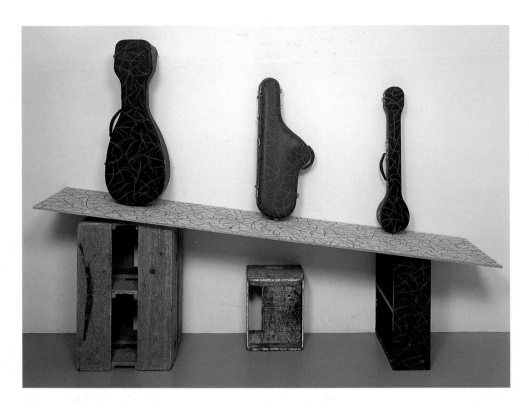

Blue Drawing, 1984
musical instrument cases,
wood boards, wooden
boxes, paint
69 x 96 x 24 inches
(175 x 244 x 61 cm)

Echo, 1984
wood, pipe, can, con-
crete, paint
74 x 136 x 312 inches
(190 x 350 x 800 cm)
Private collection

George and the Dragon,
1984
table, basket, aluminum
can, plastic piping
43 x 156 x 47 inches
(110 x 400 x 120 cm)
Arts Council Collection,
South Bank Centre,
London

Three Modern Buildings,
1984
clay and cement bricks
82 x 117 x 156 inches
(210 x 300 x 400 cm)
Private collection,
Cologne

Lens, 1985
found objects, plastic
particles

Birnan Wood, 1985
found objects, plastic
particles
51 x 74 x 82 inches
(130 x 190 x 210 cm)
Collection Eyck, Wÿlié,
The Netherlands

New Figuration, 1985
found plastic fragments
113 x 54 inches
(287 x 137 cm)
Collection J.B. Speed
Museum, Louisville,
Kentucky

Spectrum, 1985
found plastic fragments
12 x 86 x 195 inches
(30 x 220 x 500 cm)
Lisson Gallery, London

Commercial Moon, 1985
found plastic fragments
86 1/2 x 48 inches
(220 x 122 cm)
Private Collection

Bacchus Drops, 1985
wood, glass, plastic
50 3/4 x 27 1/2 x 27 1/2
inches
(130 x 70 x 70 cm)
Collection of the artist,
Wuppertal

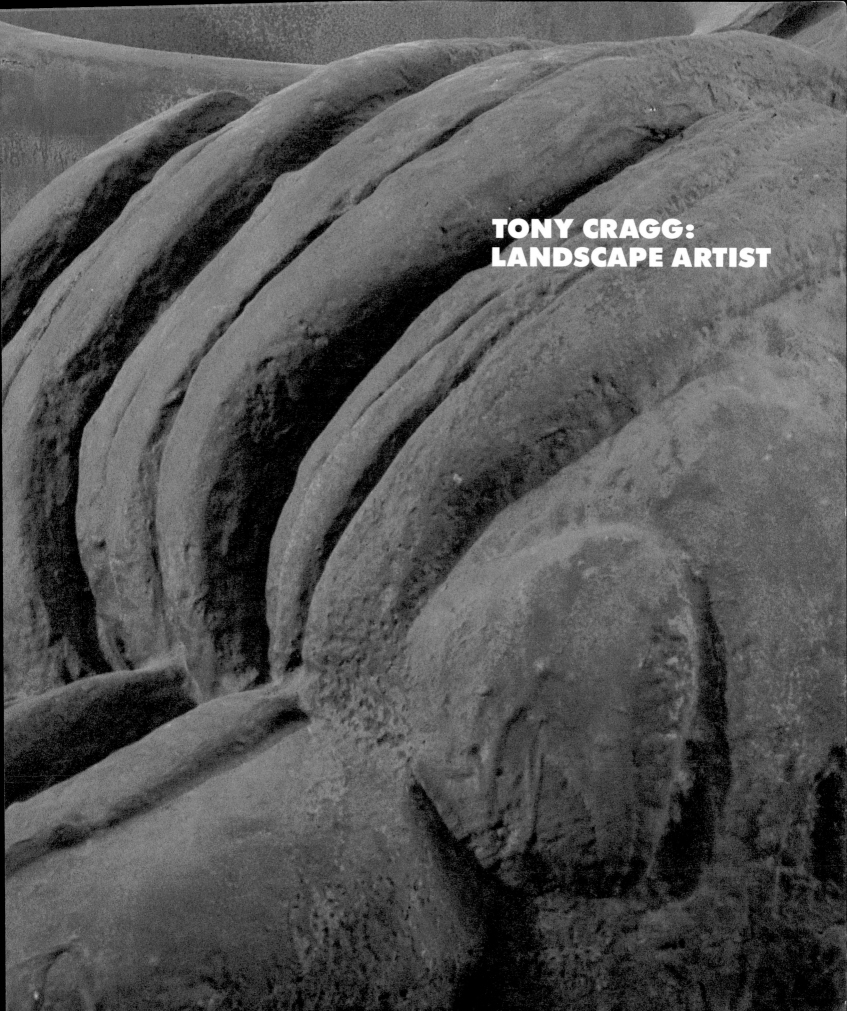

**TONY CRAGG:
LANDSCAPE ARTIST**

TONY CRAGG: LANDSCAPE ARTIST

THOMAS McEVILLEY

People say there's a great deal of variety in my work, but I'm not so sure that's true . . . . It's like making a complete landscape with all the parts in it: there's the urban world, architecture and so on, there's the organic world, there's the atmosphere, and there's the geological structure.

— Tony Cragg

Tony Cragg is an artist who changes styles, materials, formats, and contents. To some critics this has presented a problem. One suspects that their feeling is rooted in the view (central to classical modernism) that the artist deals with something like unchanging aesthetic principles.[1] If that is true, then when an artist changes his work radically he is implicitly either denouncing his past work or arousing skepticism about that to come, or both. Having found a supposed expression of universal aesthetic value, the artist had better stick with it. To change styles, in such a view, is to treat art as fashion rather than as a vehicle of unchanging verities.

Cragg seems to have a different take on the issue. He has expressed himself as feeling that the world is essentially characterized by complexity and layering; his work, as a kind of wavy mirror of the world, must reflect these traits—hence its appearance of diversity. If, however, his medley of forms portrays an integrated world, a "landscape" with its many elements, then its apparent diversity is overlaid on an underlying unity. The many parts are different limbs of a single dancer. The question of which principle—unity or diversity—is preeminent (referred to in philosophy as the "Problem of the One and the Many") runs through Cragg's oeuvre and bestows upon it a difficult balance.

Cragg's work of the early 1980s—specifically the figurative compositions in bits of found plastic detritus—embodied this problem: is the fragmented state of the materials dominant, or the temporary appearance of wholeness that rises from their composition into a recognizable representation? One solution is to allow the factor of time to suggest a cyclicity or periodicity in which fragmentation and wholeness alternate.[2] In Cragg's work the monuments and signs of civilizations (for example, *Postcard*

Float, 1986
cast iron
19 1/2 inches high x 34
1/3 inches diameter
(50 x 88 cm)
Konrad Fischer Gallery,
Düsseldorf

Model for Float
styrofoam
5 inches (13 cm) diameter

Installation at Konrad
Fischer Gallery, Munich,
1986.

Eye Bath, 1986
cast iron
21 1/2 x 22 x 16 inches
(55 x 56 x 40 cm)
Saatchi Collection,
London

hundreds of bits of plastic trash; the human figure, or self, is recognizable in its overall shape but internally fragmented, ready to become debris in its turn and then to be recycled.

Union Jack and *Britain Seen from the North*, both 1981) can be seen as shattered into tiny fragments, meaningless in themselves, which the currents of change then reassemble into new temporary meanings, or apparent wholes, which will in their turn undergo the process of disruption and decay. Civilization's debris become sedimented like a seedbed from which the future will grow.[3] The focus is on the process of change in the passage of time rather than on the thing undergoing the change. As the process builds things up and breaks them down, human selfhood becomes ambiguous, too; Cragg's *David* (1984), for example, composes an image of Michelangelo's *David* out of

The mortar and pestle works add a sexual dimension to the idea of grinding forms down into raw material and reshaping their substance. The reference to sexual intercourse points to the creative nature of what might at first glance seem a destructive process.[4] For the theme of fragmentation is closely related to—indeed a form of—the theme of transformation. The alchemist sought to reduce material form to the underlying formlessness of Prime Matter in order to make it susceptible to transformation— to erase its traits so new ones could be imposed on it. Without necessarily implying an alchemical metaphysics, Cragg's work presents a materialistic analogue of one.

The theme of fragmentation or dissolution, then, is necessary to the theme of change. It is precisely because things can lose their integrity and fragment into parts that they can be rearranged into new "selves." This primal realization tilts the balance of thought toward the Many. In our culture's first encounter with

such cruces, for example, in the pre-Socratic period, Democritus responded to Parmenides's idea of the absolute unity of Being by developing his philosophy of atomism. If things are integral wholes, they cannot change, since they cannot break up into fragments—say, molecules and atoms—to be shifted and rearranged. So the integral and unchangeable One of Parmenides had to be be broken down into the Many of Democritus in order to explain the change that so obviously occurs in the world. This process involves a sense of infinity: the infinity of molecules, the infinity of the ocean of fragments, which the artist, both parodying and embodying the idea of the Demiurge, fuses into new temporary unions.

Crackerboxes, 1986
wood
58 1/2 x 66 1/3 x 62 1/3 inches
(150 x 170 x 160 cm)
Private collection, New York

Città, 1986
hardboard, wood, paint
99 x 79 x 102 inches
(250 x 200 x 260 cm)
Saatchi Collection, London

Città, 1986
painted wood
70 x 120 x 84 inches
(177 x 305 x 213 cm)
Collection John and Mary Papajohn, Iowa

In the mid-1980s Cragg's work underwent one of its radical shifts. Gone were the plastic fragments; in their place appeared quasi-architectural sculptures of an unaccountable middle scale—too small to be habitable, too big to be architectural models. These complex, shifting, out-of-kilter volumes (such as *Als Es Wieder Warm Wurde* (1985) and *Città* (1986)) made the transition from two- to three-dimensional representation. *(Mittelschicht* (1984) was the turning point.) They also asserted wholeness as against the fragmentation of the earlier works. Specifically, they asserted the idea of a city, a momentarily whole urban-sculptural form which had risen from the shards of the past and would in turn be fragmented and sedimented for the future. In these works the pendulum of thought swung back toward the One, the idea of integration, meaning, and unity. Appropriately, since this phase of Cragg's work turned away from the theme of the fragment to the theme of the transient cultural whole, the work at this stage became less extra-studio; it involved less designating of found materials and more crafting of studio objects. The nature/culture distinction, another primal crux of human thought, began to work itself into new forms. The plastic scraps had seemed virtually parts of nature, like fallen leaves or bits of seashell on the beach; the studio-made city forms, on the other hand, seem clearly to belong to culture. But in fact the distinction is not so clear.

Critical reflections on the nature/culture dichotomy—a fundamental tenet of classical

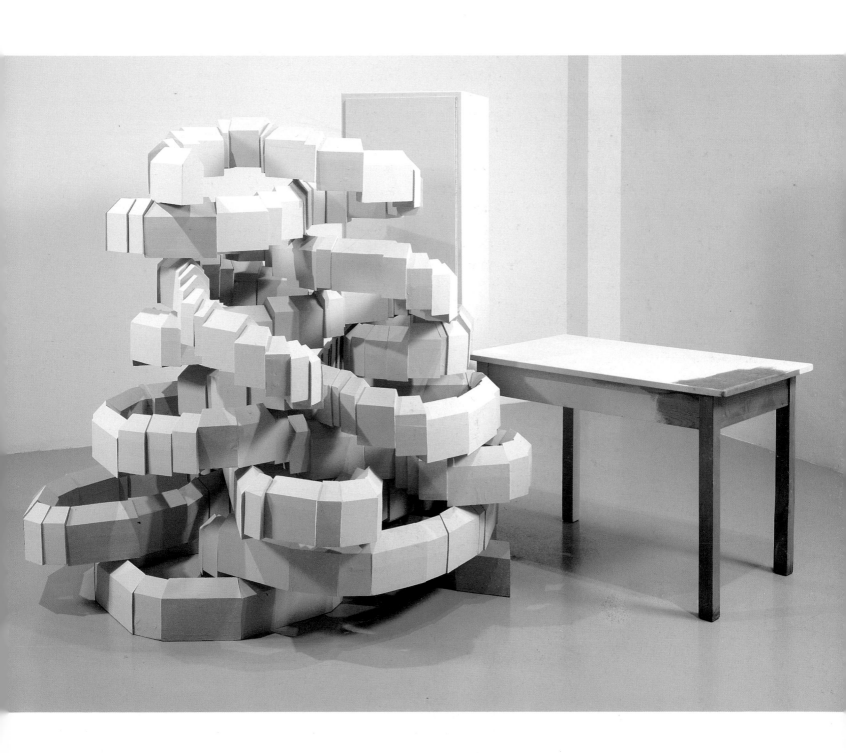

Untitled (Sugar Beets),
1987

steel and cast bronze

11 3/4 x 35 2/3 x 11 3/4

inches

(30 x 92 x 30 cm)

Radio Shacks, **1986**

granite, 4 parts

23 1/2 x 29 1/4 x 23 1/2

inches

(60 x 75 x 60 cm)

Private collection, Bern

Inverted Sugar Crop,
1986

bronze, steel

39 3/4 x 78 3/4 x 39 1/2

inches

(100 x 200 x 100 cm)

Saatchi Collection,

London

modernism[5]—are prominent throughout Cragg's oeuvre. The early eighties fragment works show culture operating as an analogue to processes of nature such as erosion, the grinding of stones into sand by the sea, the rearrangement of molecules, and so on. The mid-eighties work, with its references to more or less intact urban architecture, seems to isolate culture and focus on it as a separable category. The most recent work, finally, that of the late eighties, seems to be an even more emphatic assertion of the separateness of culture. Cast in bronze, it seems an ultimate rejection of the

plastic scraps. It echoes sculptural tradition intensely and evokes the distinction between low and high art that formal sculpture in bronze brings with it. The eighties work as a whole, then, seen in these three stages, would seem to parallel the unidirectional and progressive evolutionary idea of nature developing by stages into culture. But in Cragg's work the nature/culture distinction is never simple and clear. The plastic fragments, though they behave like nature (sand grains, leaves, things borne by wind or water into new arrangements and intentions), are in fact culture (what could be more culture than plastic?). The recent cast-bronze work is similarly ambiguous; while its material and method point to culture, its content asserts the primacy of nature. The cast bronze, then, involves not culture itself, but culture's reproduction of the nature whose product it had seemed to be. Culture and nature interpenetrate or reciprocally produce one another. *Inverted Sugar Crop* (1987), for example, involves the nature/culture dichotomy in a reciprocity or circularity; its bronzeness points to culture's representation of nature through sculpture, while its represented forms (sugar beets) point to nature as the underlying reality of culture. *Shell* (1989) shows a huge seashell lying atop the cases of modern brass instruments as if having spawned them or about to devour them. Their implied sounds seem to allude to the primal oceanic sound produced in the shell's secret inner chamber; similarly, their rounded cases, in which volumes of sound reside *in potentia*, specify the primal oceanic sound's universality. Though the natural object seems to have begotten the cultural ones, it also devours them; the instruments have arisen from nature, or the universal, and to it they return.

The three stages of Cragg's eighties work suggest a reversed linearity in another sense. The

Tools, 1986
sandstone
39 1/2 x 126 x 98 1/2
inches
(100 x 320 x 250 cm)
Saatchi Collection,
London

first, the plastic fragments, represents culture broken down and returning to nature; the second, the city forms, precedes the first conceptually, showing civilization before its shattering. The most recent phase, the cast-bronze works of the late eighties, precedes both, leaping back over the city and the naturelike process of the sedimentation of its detritus to portray the primordial level of evolutionary slime from which primal life-forms arose. Trilobites and cephalopods crawl about a prehuman sea floor and gesture toward amphibian adventures onto the land. The DNA-like spiral of *Code Noah* (1989), for example, suggests the roots of the formal coding of life. *Fruit Bottles* (1989) shows slug- or snail-like elementary life-forms, their rounded organic shapes implying primal sources of being. *Generations* (1987) depicts similar bloblike evolutionary protoforms, but here in the temporal process of reproduction. *Branchiopods* (1987) presents primal forms with phallic and mammarian connotations. *Bodicea* (1989) portrays primal inchoate beings clustering and multiplying in an amphibious transition. The work's rounded protoform is a uterine volume or vessel in which the future germinates.

The motif of the vessel, with or without paleontological associations, runs throughout Cragg's work of the eighties, from *Five Bottles on a Shelf* (1982) to *Bestückung* (1989). Echoes both in titles and in forms relate it to the theme of primordiality. *Three Cast Bottles* (1989), for example, seems to represent giant bottles washed up on a beach, relics of an unknown ancient Gargantuan civilization. *Mother's Milk II* (1988) focuses another vessel work on ideas of fertility and the source.

Yet in another sense the vessel works refer not to the distant past but to the present and the future, portraying a nature that is both eroding into endless curves and bodying forth an

unknown offspring. Above all, in regarding them we feel they involve some reference to scientific investigation. It is through science that we have become aware of the look of that primordial beginning. Acknowledging this, some of the vessels simultaneously evoke ancient goddess icons and laboratory beakers. In *Mother's Milk II* the vessel points both backward toward the primordial past viewed as a mothering vessel or source and forward into the technological or scientific future suggested by its industrial and laboratory look. In *Silence* (1988) glass vessels recalling a variety of laboratory types stand like athanors cryptically gesturing toward a future which will be born from the systematic investigation of the power of their uterine interiors; their silence is the mute anticipation of a future which, while it already resides in them *in potentia*, has not yet uttered its name or declared itself to be this or that. In *Eroded Landscape* (1987) some vessels echo classical Greek forms, others modern laboratory beakers, still others sexual organs. They evoke the passage of time, along with the fecundity of that passage and its expanding labyrinths of meanings. Cragg regards these pieces as equivalent to "figures," implying that human life is a vessel into which various experiences are poured—as various chemicals are poured into a laboratory beaker or an alchemical athanor—to be transformed not into something transcendental but into new material configurations of energy in the stream of life.

The idea of the growth of scientific knowledge is like a structural member in the work of this artist who is said to study science and to specialize in geology and fossil-gathering. Though it may seem antithetical to the themes of primordiality and regression, it is implicit in them as Cragg presents them. For it is through geological, paleontological and biological investigations that culture has recovered the

image of a primal nature from which it some-how seems to have emerged. Thus the vision of the slimy realm of cephalopods invokes the idea of progress in knowledge alongside the idea that, as the debris of culture overflow, civilization will sink back into the swamp.

It is here that the sequence of primordial thoughts in ancient philosophy again becomes relevant—specifically the way the Problem of the One and the Many led as if inevitably to the second great philosophical confrontation, the Problem of Knowledge. Fragmentation involves the theme of infinity, since there is no known limit to it. But infinity, because it contains everything, is beyond definition and distinction. In an infinity of parts there is no up or down, no forward or backward, no right or wrong. There is, in short, no meaning, since in infinity every meaning contains all others. Hence Democritus's positing of the infinity of atoms, while it loosened the world up and made room for change, led to chaos and mean-inglessness. It was followed as if inevitably by Anaxagoras' intuition of pure will in the form of Mind moving the ocean of bits and creating in it a wave and hence a direction. The idea of progress, the directional ordering of infinity, was not far behind. Cragg's apparent commit-ment to the (at least partial) reality of scientific knowledge is an analogue of the hypostatiza-tion of Mind in the midst of an ocean of material fragments. Mind gives form to the infinity of scraps; science gives meaning to the chaos of data.

In art discourse outside Great Britain Cragg more than any other artist has represented the so-called New British Sculpture of the 1980s. This category, while notoriously heterogeneous, does possess some inner coherence. Cragg's recent work, for example, resembles that of another New British Sculptor, Anish Kapoor, in

its portrayal of primordial life-forms. In different moods, both point to the foundations of the process in which life and death interpenetrate. Kapoor's approach is more metaphysical and Cragg's more materialistic. Yet Cragg's materialism does have a metaphysical or idealist aspect, which consists in the belief in science as a source of higher knowledge, knowledge which is not visual and hence is close to pure Idea.

It is here that Cragg's attitude toward history becomes ambiguous. His affirmation of pro-gress through science is classically modernist, while his affirmation of regression (implied in the fragmentation and primordialism works) is antimodern. By antimodern I mean an extreme reaction against modernism—not uncommon in the art of the late sixties and seventies—which simply inverts its values. Antimodernism, in its puritanism, seems like a disguised or inverted shadow form of modernism. In post-modernism this polarity must be balanced and resolved. Postmodernism advocates not a pure but an impure position—not in fact a position but a conflation of positions. In fact, post-modernism is not so much antimodernist as it is a modification of modernism to preserve its humane ambitions without its essentialist metaphysics and its view of history as both Eurocentric and providential. Some elements of Cragg's work achieve this postmodern resolution—for example, his combination of the theme of fragmentation with gestures towards wholeness, his acknowledgement of a very relativized and diminished metaphysics, his tendency to change styles and formats while preserving an underlying continuity of purpose. So the work is an assemblage of modernist, antimodernist, and postmodernist elements.[6]

Other Cragg works resemble Bill Woodrow's in their exclusive use of trash materials. It is not

Minster, 1987
rubber, stone, wood, metal
tallest part: 120 x 22 3/4 inches
(305 x 58 cm)
Saatchi Collection, London

Overleaf:
Riot, 1987
found plastic fragments
92 1/2 x 617 3/8 x 27 1/2 inches
(235 x 1568 x 70 cm)
Saatchi Collection, London
Installed at Hayward Gallery, 1987

Oersted Sapphire, 1987
cast aluminum
94 x 157 x 157 inches
(239 x 399 x 399 cm)
Private collection

simply that these works—with their vision of new life-forms rising from the sediment, the past recycled as a present pointing toward a future—utter a word of hope or glance toward the future, for the voice is sardonic and the eye yearns also to delight in the erasure of the world of form. The hope is combined with a *memento mori*. Each critiques and mellows the other, and the work happens somewhere in their ambiguous embrace.

Inherent in the multilayered meaning of Cragg's work is the image of the artist roaming through alleys and over beaches looking for what the rest of the world has despised and thrown away. In *Self-Portrait with Sack* (1987) the loneliness of the image is as notable as its eccentricity. The work simultaneously embodies and parodies the romantic image of the artist as a lonely adventurer seeking realms that others flee. *Self-Portrait with Sack* is an assemblage of worn, softened, and rounded plastic scraps laid on beaches as sardonic gifts of the waves and tides—*mementi mori* from the sea, as it were, pushed up by lunar phases and oceanic rhythms. With ironic circularity these shards combine to depict the artist as a wanderer with a sack, probing the trashy places where bums go, looking for the very detritus out of which his own image will be made.

NOTES

1. This transcendentalist view of art, first adumbrated (as far as extant texts go, anyway) in Plato's *Phaedrus* and Plotinus's *Enneads,* underlay Kant's *Critique of Judgement* and the whole formalist tradition of criticism that tacitly depended on that text.

2. This idea, like so much of the thematics underlying Cragg's work, goes back to the dawn of philosophy, in this case to the work of the Greek philosopher Empedocles.

3. This idea is associated with a thread of contemporary art that goes back to Robert Smithson and includes such disparate works as those of Janis Kounellis and Julian Schnabel.

4. Treating the actions of mortars and pestles or millstones as analogues of sexual interaction is ancient; it can be found, for example, in the fragments of the poet Archilochus in the 6th century BC.

5. The distinction between nature and culture as a modernist idea is above all Hegelian, but it can also be found at the roots of pre-Socratic thought, specifically in Protagoras and other Sophists.

6. See my essay "The Darkness Inside a Stone," in *Anish Kapoor,* Venice Biennale catalog (London: The British Council, 1990).

Eroded Landscape, 1987
glass, wood and steel
57 x 49 x 23 1/2 inches
(145 x 125 x 60 cm)
Private collection

Branchiopods, 1987
plaster, wood
32 x 96 x 96 inches
(81 x 244 x 244 cm)
Collection Blake Byrne,
Los Angeles

Mollusk, 1987
steel
123 x 101 x 62 inches
(312 x 257 x 158 cm)
Collection Fundacion Caja
de Pensiones, Madrid

Mortar and Pestle,
1987-88
bronze
36 x 64 x 32 inches
(90 x 160 x 80 cm)
Private collection, Japan

Spill, 1987
bronze
35 x 128 3/4 x 45 inches
(90 x 330 x 115 cm)
Collection Gerald S.
Elliott, Chicago

Bestückung, 1987-88
cast iron, 2 parts
82 x 86 x 31 1/4 inches
(210 x 220 x 80 cm)
Collection Alfred and
Mary Shands, Louisville

Mother's Milk II, 1988
bronze
35 x 75 x 55 1/2 inches
(90 x 192 x 142 cm)
Rubell Collection,
New York

Loco, 1988 (detail)
wood, 8 parts
43 1/2 x 39 1/2 x 65
inches
(111 x 99 x 165 cm)
Collection Gerald S.
Elliott, Chicago

Code Noah, 1988
bronze
129 1/2 x 39 1/3 x 39 1/3
inches
(74.9 c 99.9 x 99.9 cm)
Collection Mr. and Mrs.
Ware Travelstead,
New York

Generations, 1988
plaster, 13 parts
35 x 117 x 136 inches
(90 x 300 x 350 cm)
Courtesy Galerie Crousel-
Robelin Bama, Paris

On the Savannah, 1988
bronze
99 1/2 x 156 x 117 inches
(225 x 400 x 300 cm)
Collection Tate Gallery,
London

Three Cast Bottles, 1988
cast iron
84 x 132 2/3 x 92 2/3
inches
(215 x 340 x 240 cm)
Collection Fredrik Roos,
Malmö, Sweden

Spill, 1988 (detail)
crystal, wood
44 1/2 x 25 1/3 x 17 1/4
inches
(114 x 65 x 44 cm)
Collection Fredrik Roos,
Malmö, Sweden

Untitled (Shell), 1988
steel
43 3/8 x 86 3/4 78 3/4
inches
(110 x 220 x 200 cm)
Saatchi Collection,
London

Untitled, 1988
plaster, 10 parts
54 1/2 x 74 x 245 3/4
inches
(140 x 190 x 630 cm)
Lisson Gallery, London

Forminifera, 1988
cast and sandblasted
plaster, 4 parts
79 x 96 x 55 inches
(201 x 244 x 140 cm)
Collection Donald G.
Fisher, San Francisco

Untitled, 1988
bronze, 2 parts
Collection Musée d'Art
Moderne, Centre Georges
Pompidou, Paris

Untitled (Large Bronze),
1988
bronze
82 3/4 x 82 3/4 x 112
inches
(210 x 210 x 285 cm)
Collection The Weltkunst
Foundation, London

Branching Form, 1989
bronze
58 1/2 x 58 1/2 x 58 1/2
inches
(150 x 150 x 150 cm)
Courtesy Galerie Bernd
Klüser, Munich

Matruschka, 1989
bronze
74 x 31 x 31 inches
(190 x 80 x 80 cm)
The Rivendell Collection,
New York

Quarry 'T', 1989
cast bronze loader
40 bags of Spanish red
oxide
32 x 84 x 92 inches
(81 x 213 x 234 cm)
Courtesy Marian
Goodman Gallery,
New York

Condensor, 1989
175 1/2 x 117 x 117
inches
(450 x 300 x 300 cm)
steel
Collection of the artist,
Wuppertal

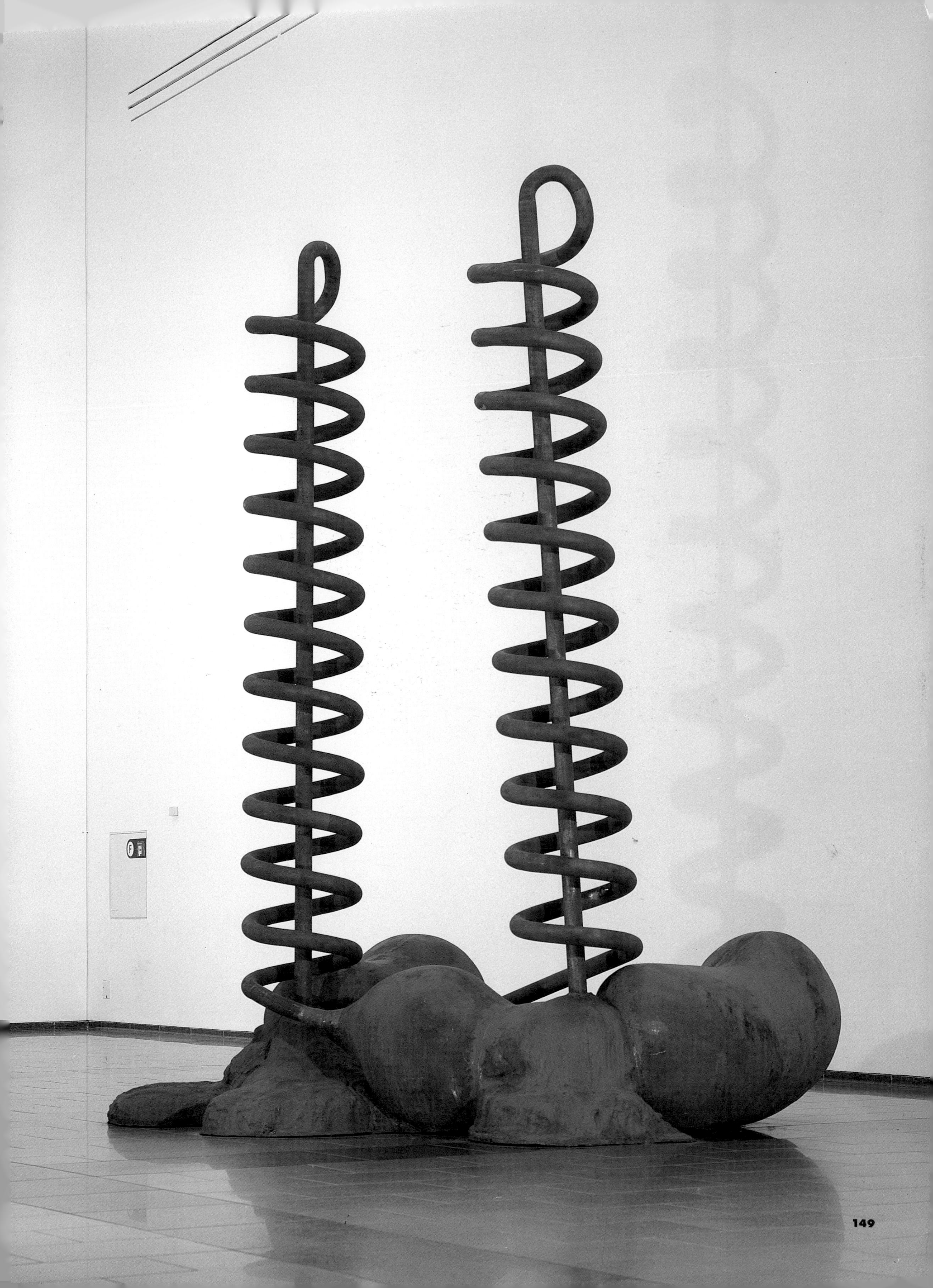

Fruit Bottles, 1989
steel, 7 parts
112 x 105 x 26 inches
(285 x 267 x 66 cm)
Private collection

Bodicea, 1989
wood, bronze, 2 parts
bronze: 31 x 70 x 25
inches
(80 x 180 x 64 cm)
wood: 9 1/2 inches
diameter x 66 1/2 inches
long
(24 x 170 cm)
Courtesy Galerie Crousel-
Robelin Bama, Paris

Sediment, 1989
marble, 9 parts
53 x 53 x 167 inches
(135 x 135 x 424 cm)
Collection The New
Academy for Art Studies,
London

Tun, 1989
granite
82 x 78 x 78 inches
(210 x 200 x 200 cm)
Collection Mr. and Mrs.
John Martin Shea,
Newport Beach,
California

Trilobites, 1989
bronze, 2 parts
78 inches high
(200 cm)
Galerie Bernd Klüser,
Munich

Untitled, 1988
sandstone
69 x 54 x 48 inches
(175 x 137 x 122 cm)
Collection Elaine and
Werner Dannheisser,
New York

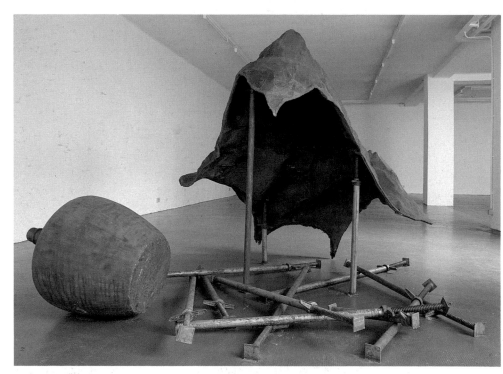

Iron Mountain, 1990
cast iron
74 x 99 1/2 x 109 inches
(190 x 255 x 280 cm)
Private collection,
courtesy Galleria Tucci
Russo, Turin

Incubation, 1990
granite
23 1/2 x 125 x 78 inches
(60 x 320 x 200 cm)
Galleria Tucci Russo,
Turin

Suburbs, 1990
wood, rubber
97 1/2 x 156 x 156 inches
(250 x 400 x 400 cm)
Collection of the artist,
Wuppertal

Untitled (Large Bronze),
1990
bronze
pipette: 117 inches high x
23 1/2 diameter
(300 x 60 cm)
bottle: 78 x 58 1/2 x 90
inches
(200 x 150 x 230 cm)
Collection of the artist,
Wuppertal

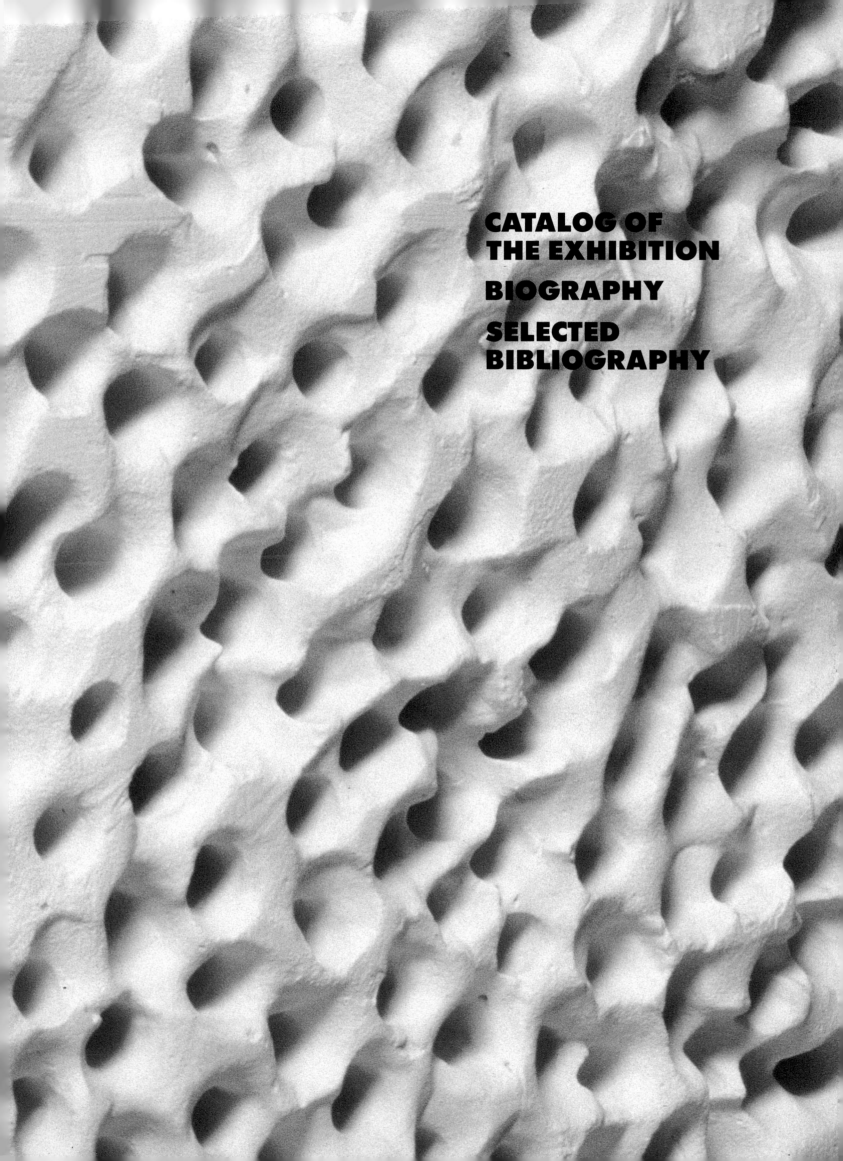

CATALOG OF
THE EXHIBITION

BIOGRAPHY

SELECTED
BIBLIOGRAPHY

CATALOG OF THE EXHIBITION

Stack, 1975/1990
mixed media
dimensions variable
Collection of the artist, Wuppertal

*New Stones—Newton's Tones, 1978
found plastic fragments
4 x 143 x 95 inches
(10 x 366 x 244 cm)
Arts Council Collection, The South Bank
Centre, London

**Newton's Tones, 1978
found plastic fragments
78 inches wide x 204 inches deep
(198 x 518 cm)
Courtesy Marian Goodman Gallery, New York

8 Flags, 1980
found plastic fragments
39 x 23 1/2 inches each
(100 x 60 cm)
Collection Angelo Baldassarre, Bari, Italy

Self-Portrait with Sack, 1980
found plastic fragments, canvas sack
67 x 25 3/4 x 15 2/3 inches
(172 x 66 x 40 cm)
Collection Sergio Bertola, Genoa

Policeman, 1981
found plastic fragments
158 x 47 inches
(401.3 x 119.4 cm)
Courtesy Lisson Gallery, London

Factory Fantasies I, 1981
cut-out wooden armoire
68 1/4 x 23 x 18 1/3 inches
(175 x 64 x 47 cm)
Fond Régional d'Art Contemporain, Rhône-
Alpes, Lyon

Rockets, 1981
found colored wood
137 x 133 inches
(348 x 337.8 cm)
Courtesy Galerie Bernd Klüser, Munich

Five Bottles on a Shelf, 1982
plastic
13 x 23 x 5 1/2 inches
(33 x 58.4 x 14 cm)
Collection Donald Young, Chicago

Large Window III, 1983
white paint on found colored wood
106 x 80 inches
(269.2 x 203.2 cm)
Collection James N. and Susan A. Phillips,
Playa del Rey, California

Small Landscape, 1983
stone, wood
25 3/4 x 33 1/2 x 12 1/2 inches
(66 x 86 x 32 cm)
Private collection, Turin

Two Positions, 1983
wood furniture, stone
37 1/2 x 62 1/2 x 62 1/2 inches
(95.2 x 158.7 x 158.7 cm)
Collection Anne and Martin Z. Margulies,
Miami

African Culture Myth, 1984
found plastic fragments
164 x 39 inches
(420 x 100 cm)
Collection Kunstmuseum Luzern, Lucerne

Silent Place with Dwelling, 1984
wood
61 x 41 x 23 1/2 inches
(155 x 105 x 60 cm)
Collection Nagoya City Art
Museum, Nagoya

Bacchus Drops, 1985
wood, glass, plastic
50 3/4 x 27 1/2 x 27 1/2 inches
(130 x 70 x 70 cm)
Collection of the artist, Wuppertal

Eye Bath, 1986
cast iron
21 1/2 x 22 x 16 inches
(55 x 56 x 40 cm)
Saatchi Collection, London

Inverted Sugar Crop, 1986
bronze, steel
39 3/8 x 78 3/4 x 39 3/8 inches
(100 x 200 x 100 cm)
Saatchi Collection, London

Branchiopods, 1987
plaster, wood
32 x 96 x 96 inches
(81.3 x 243.8 x 243.8 cm)
Collection Blake Byrne, Los Angeles

Minster, 1987
rubber, stone, wood, metal
82 1/4 x 31 1/2 inches
(209 x 80 cm)
120 x 22 3/4 inches
(305 x 58 cm)
76 3/4 x 19 3/4 inches
(195 x 50 cm)
90 1/2 x 17 3/4 inches
(230 x 45 cm)
118 1/4 x 30 3/4 inches
(300 x 78 cm)
Saatchi Collection, London

Riot, 1987
found plastic fragments
92 1/2 x 617 3/8 x 27 1/2 inches
(234.9 x 1568.1 x 69.8 cm)
Saatchi Collection, London

Mortar and Pestle, 1987-88
bronze
36 x 64 x 32 inches
(92 x 162 x 81 cm)
Private collection, Japan

Code Noah, 1988
bronze
129 1/2 x 39 1/3 x 39 1/3 inches
(75 x 100 x 100 cm)
Collection Mr. and Mrs. Ware Travelstead,
New York

Loco, 1988
wood
43 1/2 x 39 1/2 x 65 inches
(110.5 x 99.9 x 165.1 cm)
Collection Gerald S. Elliott, Chicago

Mother's Milk II, 1988
bronze
35 x 75 x 55 1/2 inches
(90 x 192 x 142 cm)
Rubell Collection, New York

Generations, 1988
plaster
35 x 117 x 136 inches
(90 x 300 x 350 cm)
Courtesy Galerie Crousel-Robelin Bama, Paris

Untitled, 1988
sandstone
69 x 54 x 48 inches
(175 x 137 x 122 cm)
Collection Elaine and Werner Dannheisser,
New York

Untitled (Large Bronze), 1988
bronze
82 3/4 x 82 3/4 x 112 inches
(210.2 x 210.2 x 284.5 cm)
Collection The Weltkunst Foundation, London

Untitled (Shell), 1988
steel
43 3/8 x 86 3/4 x 78 3/4 inches
(110.1 x 220.3 x 200 cm)
Saatchi Collection, London

Tun, 1989
granite
82 x 78 x 78 inches
(210 x 200 x 200 cm)
Collection Mr. and Mrs. John Martin Shea,
Newport Beach, California

Bodicea, 1989
wood, bronze
bronze: 31 1/4 x 70 1/4 x 25 inches
(80 x 180 x 64 cm)
wood: 9 1/2 x 66 1/2 inches
(24 x 170 cm)
Courtesy Galerie Crousel-Robelin Bama, Paris

Condensor, 1989
steel
175 1/2 x 117 x 117 inches
(450 x 300 x 300 cm)
Collection of the artist, Wuppertal

Quarry 'T,' 1989
cast bronze loader,
40 bags Spanish red oxide
32 x 84 x 92 inches
(81 x 213 x 234 cm)
Courtesy Marian Goodman Gallery, New York

Suburbs, 1990
wood, rubber
97 1/2 x 156 x 156 inches
(250 x 400 x 400 cm)
Collection of the artist, Wuppertal

Plow, 1990
cast iron, bronze
58 1/2 x 39 x 31 1/4 inches
(150 x 100 x 80 cm)
Courtesy Marian Goodman
Gallery, New York

Untitled (Large Bronze), 1990
bronze
pipette: 117 inches high x 23 1/2 inches
diameter (300 x 60 cm)
bottle: 78 x 58 1/2 x 90 inches
(200 x 150 x 230 cm)
Collection of the artist, Wuppertal

*first venue only
**every venue except first

BIOGRAPHY

Born in Liverpool, 1949. Lab technician at the Natural Rubber Producers Research Association, 1966-68. Attended Gloucester College of Art and Design, Cheltenham, and Wimbledon School of Art, 1968-72. Attended Royal College of Art, 1973-77. M.A. at the Royal College of Art, 1977. Has lived in Wuppertal, West Germany, since 1977.

SELECTED SOLO EXHIBITIONS

1990   Crown Point Press, San Francisco
       Galerie Buchmann, Basel
       Tucci Russo, Turin

1989   Marian Goodman, New York
       Konrad Fischer, Düsseldorf
       Kanransha Gallery, Tokyo
       Kunstsammlung Nordrhein-Westfalen, Düsseldorf
       Tate Gallery, London
       Thomas Cohn, Rio de Janeiro
       Stedelijk Van Abbe Museum, Eindhoven

1988   Venice Biennale
       Galerie Marga Paz, Madrid
       Galerie Buchmann, Basel
       Galerie Crousel-Robelin, Paris
       Foksal Gallery, Warsaw
       Lisson Gallery, London
       Silo, Val de Valse

1987   Hayward Gallery, London
       Corner House, Manchester
       Tucci Russo, Turin
       Kanransha Gallery, Tokyo
       Marian Goodman, New York

1986   Galerie Buchmann, Basel
       Joost Declercq, Ghent
       The Brooklyn Museum, Brooklyn
       Marian Goodman, New York

University Art Museum, University of California, Berkeley
Geward, Ghent
La Jolla Museum of Contemporary Art, La Jolla, California
Pierre Huber, Geneva
Konrad Fischer, Düsseldorf

1985   Kunsthalle Waaghaus, Winterthur
       Staatsgalerie Moderner Kunst, Munich
       Donald Young Gallery, Chicago
       Lisson Gallery, London
       Art & Project, Amsterdam
       Palais des Beaux-Arts, Brussels
       ARC, Musée d'Art Moderne de la Ville de Paris
       Galerie Bernd Klüser, Munich
       Kestner-Gesellschaft, Hannover

1984   Yarlow & Salzmann, Toronto
       De Vlesshal, Middleburg, Holland
       Louisiana Museum of Modern Art, Humlebaek, Denmark
       Schellman & Klüser, Munich
       Marian Goodman, New York
       Kanransha Gallery, Tokyo
       Crousel-Hussenot, Paris
       Kölnischer Kunstverein, Cologne
       Tucci Russo, Turin

1983   Lucio Amelio, Naples
       Marian Goodman, New York
       Kunsthalle Bern
       Art & Project, Amsterdam
       Thomas Cohn, Rio de Janeiro
       Galerie Buchmann, St. Gallen
       Franco Toselli, Milan

1982   Badischer Kunstverein, Karlsruhe
       Kanransha Gallery, Tokyo
       Nisshin Gallery, Tokyo
       Marian Goodman, New York

Nouveau Musée, Lyon
Chantal Crousel, Paris
Büro Berlin
Schellmann & Klüser, Munich
Lisson Gallery, London
Konrad Fischer, Düsseldorf
Rijksmuseum Kröller-Müller, Otterloo

1981   Schellmann & Klüser, Munich
Musée d'Art et d'Industrie, St. Etienne
Whitechapel Art Gallery, London
Nouveau Musée, Lyon
Front Room, London
Von der Heydt Museum, Wuppertal
Vacuum, Düsseldorf

1980   Arnolfini Gallery, Bristol
Konrad Fischer, Düsseldorf
Lisson Gallery, London
Chantal Crousel, Paris
Lützowstrasse Situation, Berlin
Lucio Amelio, Naples
Franco Toselli, Milan
Saman Gallery, Genoa

1979   Lisson Gallery, London
Lützowstrasse Situation, Berlin
Künstlerhaus Weidenallee, Hamburg

SELECTED GROUP EXHIBITIONS

1990   *A Group Show*, Marian Goodman
Gallery, New York
Signs of Life, Institute of Contemporary
Art, University of Pennsylvania,
Philadelphia
Von der Natur in der Kunst,
Messepalast, Vienna
*Culture and Commentary: An '80s
Perspective*, Hirshhorn Museum and
Sculpture Garden, Washington, D.C.

The Biennale of Sydney, Art Gallery of
New South Wales, Sydney

1989   *Britse Sculptuur 1960/1988 British
Sculpture*, Museum van Hedendaagse
Kunst, Antwerp
Subject : Object, Nicola Jacobs and
Donald Young Galleries, Chicago
The European Avant-Garde, Freedman
Gallery, Albright College, Reading,
Pennsylvania

1988   *Présentation & Propositions*, FRAC
Rhône-Alpes, Ville du Parc
De Verzameling, Museum van
Hedendaagse Kunst, Antwerp
*Britannica: Vingt-Cinq Ans de
Sculpture*, Musée des Beaux-Arts André
Malraux, Le Havre
Camouflage, Scottish Arts Council,
Third Eye Centre, Glasgow; traveled
*Starlit Waters: British Sculpture, An
International Art, 1968-1988*, Tate
Gallery, Liverpool

1987   *Current Affairs: British Painting and
Sculpture in the 1980s*, British
Council; traveled in Hungary,
Czechoslovakia, and Poland
*The Quiet Revolution: British Sculpture
Since 1965*, Museum of Contemporary
Art, Chicago; traveled
British Art of the 1980s, Liljevalchs
Konsthall, Stockholm; traveled as
Britannica to the Sara Hilden Art
Museum, Tampere, Finland
L'époque, la mode, la moral, la passion,
Musée d'Art Moderne, Centre Georges
Pompidou, Paris
Anderer Leute Kunst, Museum Haus
Lange, Krefeld

Juxtapositions, P.S.1, The Institute for
   Art and Urban Resources, Long Island
   City, New York
Documenta 8, Kassel
Drawing, Kanransha Gallery, Tokyo
Edinburgh International, Royal Scottish
   Academy, Edinburgh

1986 *The Generic Figure*, Corcoran Gallery of
   Art, Washington, D.C.
Venice Biennale
Beuys zu Ehren, Städtische Galerie im
   Lenbachhaus, Munich
Entre el objecto y la imagen, Palacio de
   Velázquez, Madrid; traveled
*Echo und Monumente Ihrer Präzisen
   Reise*, Kunsthaus, Zurich
Englische Bildhauer, Galerie Harold
   Behm, Hamburg
De Sculptura, Vienna
Skulptur Sein, Städtische Kunsthalle,
   Düsseldorf
Sonsbeek '86, Arnheim

1985 *Aureola Borealis*, Oslo
*Turner Prize Exhibition of Shortlisted
   Artists*, Tate Gallery, London
7000 Eichen, Kunsthalle Tübingen
*Die sich verselbständigenden Möbel —
   Objekte und Installationen von
   Künstlern*, Von der Heydt Museum,
   Wuppertal
18th Biennale, Antwerp
Alles und noch viel mehr, Kunsthalle
   Bern
Anniottanta, Galleria Comunale d'Arte
   Moderna, Bologna
The British Show, Art Gallery of Western
   Australia, Perth; traveled
Hayward Annual, Hayward Gallery,
   London

1984 *Sol-Mur*, Musée des Beaux-Arts, Rouen
Plastiques et Plasticiens, Zem,
   Martigues
Tilt l'Art à l'Oeuvre, Musée de Nantes,
   Nantes
The Biennale of Sydney, Art Gallery of
   New South Wales, Sydney
*An International Survey of Recent
   Painting and Sculpture*, Museum of
   Modern Art, New York
Histoire de sculpture, Château des Ducs
   d'Eperon, Cadillac; traveled
Skulptur im 20. Jahrhundert, Merian
   Park, Basel
Anzinger, Cragg, Lavier, Galerie
   Buchmann, Basel
The British Art Show, British Arts
   Council; traveled
ROSC, The Guinness Hop Store, Dublin

1983 *Truc et Troc, Lecons des Choses*, ARC,
   Musée d'Art Moderne de la Ville de
   Paris
*Pierre et Marie, Une exposition en
   traveau*, Institut Curie, Paris
Terremoto, Istituto per l'Arte
   Contemporanea, Naples
Sculpture 1983, Kunststichting,
   Rotterdam
*Boltanski, Cragg, Cucchi, Disler,
   McLean, Sherman*, Crousel-Hussenot,
   Paris
The Sculpture Show, Hayward and
   Serpentine Galleries, London
*Transformations—New Sculpture from
   Britain*, XVII Bienal de São Paulo;
   traveled
Arcaico Contemporaneo, Museo del
   Sannio, Benevento
Ars '83, Kunstmuseet Ateneum, Helsinki
Summer Show, Kanransha Gallery,
   Tokyo

Figures and Objects, John Hansard
Gallery, Southampton
La Trottola di Sirio, Centro d'Arte
Contemporaneo, Syracuse
New Art, Tate Gallery, London

1982 *Aspects of British Art Today*,
Metropolitan Museum, Tokyo;
traveled
Indian Triennale, New Delhi
De la Catastrophe, Centre d'art
Contemporain, Geneva
Art and Architecture, Institute of
Contemporary Art, London
Neue Skulptur, Nächst St. Stephan,
Vienna
Documenta 7, Kassel
*Englische Plastik Heute/British
Sculpture Now*, Kunsthalle Luzern
Leçons des Choses, Kunsthalle Bern;
traveled
Kunst im öffentlichen Raum, Musée
Savoisien, Chambéry
Kunst wird Material, Neue
Nationalgalerie, Berlin
Objects and Figures, Fruitmarket
Gallery, Edinburgh

1981 *Enciclopedia*, Museum of Contemporary
Art, Modena
Through the Summer, Lisson Gallery,
London
The Motor Show, Front Room, London
*British Sculpture in the Twentieth
Century*, Whitechapel Art Gallery,
London

1980 *B. Meadows at the Royal College of Art*,
Cambridge
Nouva Immagine, Triennale, Milan
A Perspective, Basel

Aperto '80, Venice Biennale
Kunst in Europa na '68, Museum van
Hedendaagse Kunst, Ghent

1979 *Summer Show*, Lisson Gallery, London
Europa-Kunst der 80er Jahre, Stuttgart

1978 *JA-NA-PA III*, Paris

1977 Lisson Gallery, London
Fine Arts Building, New York
RCA Degree Show, Royal College of Art,
London
Silver Jubilee Sculpture Show, Battersea
Park, London

1976 Ecole des Beaux-Arts, Metz

1975 Brunel University, Uxbridge
Royal College of Art, Gulbenkian Hall,
London

BIBLIOGRAPHY

CATALOGS

Arcaico Contemporaneo, con Tony Cragg, Mario Merz, Bill Woodrow. Benevento, Italy: Museo del Sannio, 1983. Essay by Enrico Comi.

Aspects of British Art Today. Tokyo and London: Metropolitan Art Museum and The British Council. Essay by David Brown.

Beelden/Sculpture 1983. Rotterdam: Rotterdam Arts Council, 1983. Essay by Paul Heftig.

British Art of the 1980s. Stockholm: Lilejevalchs Konsthall, 1987.

British Sculpture in the Twentieth Century. London: Whitechapel Art Gallery, 1981. Essay by F. Crichton.

The British Show. Perth, Australia: Art Gallery of Western Australia and The British Council, 1985. Essay by Michael Newman.

Britse Sculptuur 1960/1988 British Sculpture. Antwerp: Museum van Hedendaagse Kunst, 1989. Essay by Lynne Cooke.

Documenta 7. Catalogs 1 and 2. Kassel: Documenta 7, 1982.

Enciclopedia del Magico Primario en Europa. Modena, Spain: Galería Civica, 1981. Essay by Ursula Peters.

Englische Plastik Heute/British Sculpture Now: Stephen Cox, Tony Cragg, Richard Deacon, Anish Kapoor, Bill Woodrow. Lucerne, Switzerland: Kunstmuseum Luzern, 1982. Essay by Michael Newman.

Entre el objeto y la imagen: escultura Británica contemporáneo. Madrid and London, Ministerio de Cultura and The British Council, 1986.

Kunst in Europa na '68. Ghent: Museum van Hedendaagse Kunst, 1981.

Leçon des Choses. Bern, Switzerland, and Chambéry, France: Kunsthalle Bern and Musée Savoisien, 1982. Interview by Jean-Hubert Martin.

Nature as Material. London: Arts Council of Great Britain, n.d. (1980). Essay by A. Causey.

New British Art in the Saatchi Collection. London: Thames and Hudson. Essays by Alistair Hicks.

Nouva Immagine/New Image. Milan: XVI Triennale, 1980. Essay by Flavio Caroli.

Objects and Figures. Edinburgh: Fruitmarket Gallery and Scottish Arts Council, 1982.

A Quiet Revolution: British Sculpture Since 1965. Chicago: Museum of Contemporary Art, 1987.

The Sculpture Show: Fifty Sculptors at the Serpentine and at the South Bank. London: Arts Council of Great Britain, 1983. Essays by Fenella Crichton, Kate Blacker, Paul de Monchaux.

Starlit Waters, British Sculpture and International Art 1968-88. Liverpool: Tate Gallery, 1988. Essay by Lynne Cooke.

Tema Celeste. Gibellina: Museo Civico d'Arte Contemporaneo di Gibellina, 1983. Essay by Demetrio Paparoni.

Tony Cragg. Bern: Kunsthalle Bern, 1983. Essays by Jean-Hubert Martin and Germano Celant.

Tony Cragg. Düsseldorf: Kunstsammlung Nordrhein-Westfalen, 1989.

Tony Cragg: Skulpturen. Hannover: Kestner-Gesellschaft, 1986. Essays by Tony Cragg, Demosthènes Davvetas, Carl Haenlein.

Tony Cragg. Karlsruhe: Badischer Kunstverein, 1982. Essay by Michael Newman.

Tony Cragg. London: Arts Council of Great Britain and Hayward Gallery, 1987. Essay and interview by Lynne Cooke.

Tony Cragg. London: The British Council, 1982. Published for the Indian Triennial. Essays by Norbert Lynton and J. Andrews.

Tony Cragg. London: The British Council, 1988. Published for the XLIII Venice Biennale. Essays by Catherine Lampert and Demosthènes Davvetas.

Tony Cragg. Saint-Etienne: Musée d'Art et d'Industrie, 1981. Essay by Bernard Ceysson.

Tony Cragg. St. Gallen and de Vleeshal: Galerie Buchmann, 1983. Essay by Armin Wildermuth.

Tony Cragg. Bern: Galerie Buchmann, 1990. Essay by Armin Wildermuth.

Tony Cragg. Tokyo: Kanransha Gallery, 1984. Essay by Reiji Kawaguchi.

Tony Cragg. Tokyo: Kanransha Gallery, 1982. Essay by Nobrou Nakamura.

Tony Cragg. Turin: Galleria Antonio Tucci Russo, 1984.

Tony Cragg. Wuppertal: Von der Heydt Museum, 1981. Essay by Ursula Peters.

Tony Cragg. Brussels: Société des Expositions du Palais des Beaux-Arts, 1985. Essay by Annelie Pohlen, interview with Demosthènes Davvetas.

Tony Cragg's 'Axehead.' London: The Tate Gallery, 1984. Essay by Pat Turner.

Tony Cragg: Sculptures. Ardenne: Ministère de la Culture/FRAC Champagne, et al., 1988.

Tony Cragg, Vier Arbeiten. Köln: Kölnischer Kunstverein, 1984.

Tony Cragg: Winner of the 1988 Turner Prize. London: Tate Gallery and Patrons of New Art, 1988.

Transformations: New Sculpture from Britain. London: The British Council, 1983. Published for the XVII Bienal de São Paulo. Essays by Nicholas Serota and John Roberts.

ARTICLES

Allthorpe-Guyton, M. "Tony Cragg." *Flash Art* no. 134 (May 1987):76.

Annear, Judy, and Harrison, Charles. *Art Monthly* (May 1985).

Archer, Michael. "Tony Cragg, Lisson Gallery." *Artforum* 27, no. 8 (April 1989):180.

Artner, Alan G. "Sculptors Appeal to the Eye— Through the Mind." *Chicago Tribune* (21 March 1985).

Baker, Kenneth. "Tony Cragg at Marian Goodman." *Art in America* 72, no. 8 (September 1984):206.

Beaumont, Mary Rose. "Beyond Tradition: Sculpture since Caro." *Art and Design* (U.K.) 3, no. 1/2 (February 1987):68-73.

——— . "Kassel: Documenta 7." *Arts Review* (U.K.) 34, no. 15 (16 July 1982):385.

——— . "Tony Cragg, Lisson Gallery." *Arts Review* (U.K.) 37, no. 7 (12 April 1985):177.

Besson, Christian. "Tony Cragg." *Public* no. 1.

Bickers, Patricia. "New Models for Old: Tony Cragg at the 43rd Venice Biennale." *Art Monthly* (September 1988).

Biggs, Lewis. "Tony Cragg." *Arnolfini Review* (Bristol, England) (May/June 1980):n.p.

Bischoff, U. "Sculptur im 20. Jahrhundert." *Pantheon* 42, no. 4 (October/December 1984):390.

Bloch, Patrice, and Pesenti, Laurent. "Nouvelle sculpture: la culture de l'objet." *Beaux Arts Magazine* no. 3 (June 1983):40-45.

Bonaventura, Paul. "An Introduction to Recent British Sculpture." *Artefactum* (Belgium) 4, no. 20 (September/October 1987):3-7, 67-72.

Bowen, Lisa Balfour. "Venice: Sculpture Dominates the 43rd Venice Biennale." *Artpost* (Canada) 6, no. 1 (Fall 1988):28-30.

Braxmeier, Rainer. "Tony Cragg, Badischer Kunstverein, Karlsruhe." *Kunstwerk* 35, no. 2 (April 1982):71.

Brighton, Andrew. *Art Monthly* (December/ January 1984-85).

Bumpus, Judith. "Tony Cragg, Hayward Gallery." *Arts Review* (U.K.) 39, no. 5 (13 March 1987):158.

Camnitzer, Luis. "La XLIII Bienal de Venecia en sus 93 años." *Arte en Columbia* (Columbia) no. 38 (December 1988):53-57, 137-38.

Castello, Michelangelo. "Sculpting Memory: Tony Cragg." *Tema Celeste* no. 22/23 (October/ December 1989):62-65.

Celant, Germano. "Dall'Alfa Trainer allo Subway." *Segno* (28 September 1982).

——— . "Tony Cragg and Industrial Platonism." *Artforum* 20, no. 3 (November 1981):40-46.

Cooke, Lynne. "Darkling Light." *Parkett* no. 18 (1988):96-102.

——— . "Reconsidering the 'New Sculpture.'" *Artscribe* no. 42 (August 1983):25-29.

——— . "Tony Cragg at the Whitechapel." *Artscribe* no. 28 (March 1981):54-55.

Cragg, Tony. *Artforum* 26, no. 7 (March 1988):120-22. Project for *Artforum*.

Cuvelier, Pascaline. "Le Système anglo-panique des objets, Tony Cragg: objets perdus." *Libération* (4 May 1982):24-25.

Davvetas, Demosthènes. "Tony Cragg: bris d'images." *Beaux Arts Magazine* no. 57 (May 1988):36-41.

DeVuono, F. *Art News* 89 (February 1990):153.

Dimitriejevic, Nena. "Sculpture after Evolution." *Flash Art* no. 117 (April/May 1984):28.

Duthy, Robin. "Not for the Sofa Table." *Connoisseur* 214, no. 866 (April 1984):79-80.

"Echt Plastik." *Der Spiegel* (12 March 1984).

Feaver, William. "It's New Because It's New." *Art News* 83, no. 1 (January 1984):120.

——— . "The New British Sculpture." *Art News* 83, no. 1 (January 1984):71-75.

——— . "Totter and a Pearly King." *Observer* (London) (8 March 1987):26.

Ferbos, Catherine. "Sculptures 'in-between'—le paysage." *Artstudio* (France) no. 10 (Autumn 1988):20-25.

Frehner, Matthias. "Eindrücke von der XLIII Biennale in Venedig." *Kunstbulletin des Scweizerischen Kunstvereins* (Switzerland) no. 9 (September 1988):4-9.

Gintz, Claude. "La sculpture et ses objets: l'objet de la sculpture." *Art Press* (France) no. 66 (January 1983):24-27.

Godfrey, Tony. "Tony Cragg." *Burlington Magazine* 129, no. 1010 (May 1987):337.

Goldman, Leah. "Tony Cragg, La Jolla Museum of Contemporary Art." *Art News* 86, no. 1 (January 1987):62.

Graham-Dixon, Andrew. "Cragg's Way." *Art News* 88, no. 3 (March 1989):132-37.

——— . "Great Britain Neo, No: Still Faithful to the Old Guard." *Art News* 88, no. 7 (September 1989):122-26.

Groot, Paul. "'Sculpture '83,' Rotterdam Art Foundation." *Artforum* 22, no. 1 (September 1983):83.

Heartney, Eleanor. "Born Again Objects." *Art in America* 76, no. 3 (March 1988):107-15.

Hegewisch, K. *Kunstwerk* 37 (June 1984):88-89.

Hennessey, William. J. "Reflections on the 39th Venice Biennale." *Art Journal* 41, no. 1 (Spring 1981):72.

Higgins, Judith. "Britain's New 'New Generation.'" *Art News* 86, no. 10 (December 1987):118-22.

Idone, Carol. "Sculpture in the 20th Century, Merian-Park, Basel." *Flash Art* no. 119 (November 1984):46-47.

Jones, Ben. "A New Wave in Sculpture: A Survey of Recent Work by Ten Younger Sculptors." *Artscribe* no. 8 (September 1977):14-19.

Kirshner, Judith Russi. "Tony Cragg, Richard Deacon." *Artforum* 23, no. 10 (Summer 1985):113.

Lemaître, Isabelle. "Interview with Tony Cragg." *Artefactum* (Belgium) 2, no. 11 (November-December 1985):7-11.

Lewallen, Constance. "Tony Cragg." *View* (Point Publications, San Francisco) 6, no. 1 (Winter 1989). Entire issue devoted to Tony Cragg.

Linker, Kate. "Tony Cragg, Marian Goodman Gallery." *Artforum* 26, no. 6 (February 1988):146-47.

Lynn, V. "New British Sculpture." *Art and Australia* (Australia) 23, no. 2 (Summer 1985):226-30.

Madoff, Steven Henry. "Venice Biennale: Calm Waters." *Art News* 87, no. 7 (September 1988):178-80.

Martin, Henry. "A Letter from Paris." *Art International* (Switzerland) 42, no. 3/4 (November/December 1980):45-46.

Martin, Rupert. "Tony Cragg, Lisson, London." *Flash Art* no. 145 (March/April 1989):121.

Maubant, Jean-Louis. "Découpage/Collage, à propos de Tony Cragg." *Cahiers du cric* (Le Nouveau Musée/NDLR, Lyon) 4 (May 1982).

McDonald, Robert. "Small But Choice La Jolla Exhibition." *Los Angeles Times* (5 September 1986).

McEwen, John. "Tony Cragg at the Hayward." *Art in America* 75, no. 7 (July 1987):36-37.

McManus, Michael. "The Composite Antistylist." *Artweek* 17 (6 September 1986):5.

Morgan, Stuart. "James Coleman, Nigel Greenwood Gallery; Tony Cragg, Lisson Gallery." *Artforum* 19, no. 2 (October 1980):85-86.

Museumjournaal (Stedelijk Van Abbemuseum, Holland) 34, no. 2/3 (1989).

Newman, Michael. "Discourse and Desire: Recent British Sculpture." *Flash Art* no. 115 (January 1984):48-55.

——— . "Figuren und Objekte: Neue Skulptur in England." *Kunstforum International* 62 (June 1983):22.

——— . "Man's Place: Four Works." *Art and Artists* no. 193 (October 1982):35-37.

——— . "New Sculpture in Britain." *Art in America* 70, no. 8 (September 1982):104-14, 177-79.

Norrie, Jane. "Tony Cragg, Tate Gallery." *Arts Review* (U.K.) 41, no. 10 (19 May 1989):384.

Overy, Paul. "The Britishness of Sculpture." *Studio International* (U.K.) no. 1018 (November 1987):8-13.

Peters, Philip. "Een tank van telfoonboeken, wat moet een mens ermee?" *De Tijd* (7 January 1983):38.

Petzal, Monica. "Bruce McLean/Tony Cragg/English Expressionism." *Art Monthly* no. 86 (May 1985):18-19.

Phelps, Edward. "Joel Degen, Tony Cragg, Bruce McLean: Arnolfini Gallery." *Arts Review* (U.K.) 32, no. 13 (4 July 1980):289.

Piguet, Philippe. "Val de Vesle, Tony Cragg." *L'Oeil: revue d'art* no. 396/397 (July/August 1988):68.

Pincus, Robert L. "One Man's Discards Another Man's Art in La Jolla." *San Diego Union* (28 August 1986).

Pohlen, Annelie. "Hiroshima und danach." *Kunstforum International* (February 1983):178-85.

——— . "Skulptur '85, Von der Magie der Dinge und Stoffe vom alltäglichen Gift, Mit Statements von Tony Cragg." *Kunstforum International* 79 (May/June 1985):156-84.

——. "Tony Cragg, Kestner-Gesellschaft." *Artforum* 24, no. 9 (May 1986):148-49.

Politi, Giancarlo. "Interview with Nicholas Logsdail." *Flash Art* no. 120 (January 1985):34-35.

Ponti, Lisa. "Tony Cragg." *Domus* no. 611 (November 1980):50-51.

Porges, Maria. "Tracing a Different Path: A Survey of Recent British Sculpture." *Artweek* 18, no. 25 (11 July 1987):1.

Princenthal, Nancy. "Tony Cragg at Marian Goodman." *Art in America* 74, no. 6 (June 1986):127.

"Prints and Photographs Published." *Print Collectors Newsletter* 19 (January/February 1989):228.

Puvogel, Renate. "Tony Cragg." *Kunstforum International* 102 (August 1989):316.

——. "Tony Cragg." *Künstler Kritisches Lexikon der Gegenwartskunst*. Munich: Weltkunst and Bruckmann, 1989.

Roberts, John. "Urban Renewal (New British Sculpture)." *Parachute* (Montreal) no. 30 (March 1983).

Rogozinski, Luciana. "Tony Cragg, Galleria Tucci Russo." *Artforum* 23, no. 7 (March 1985):107.

Schmidt-Wulffen, Stephan. "Tony Cragg, British Pavilion." *Flash Art* no. 142 (October 1988): 107-08.

Semin, Didier. "Tony Cragg: des outils pour la pensée." *Art Press* (France) no. 116 (July/August 1987):22-25.

Stanislawski, Krzysztof. "Aspekty rzeźby (1)." *Sztuka* (Poland) 12, no. 3 (1987):14-19.

Stellweg, Carla. "Tony Cragg: Marian Goodman." *Art News* 82, no. 6 (1983):194.

Sterckx, Pierre. "Tony Cragg: présentation de la sculpture." *Artstudio* (France) no. 10 (Autumn 1988):104-19.

Strasser, Catherine. "Tony Cragg, Galerie Chantal Crousel." *Flash Art* no. 100 (November 1980):50.

Stutzer, Beat. "Englische Plastik Heute." *Pantheon* 40, no. 3 (July/August/September 1982):258.

Tallman, Susan. "Laboratory Still Lives: 35 Prints by Tony Cragg." *Arts Magazine* 63, no. 6 (February 1989):17-18.

Taylor, Sue. "Scavenging Artists Send a Message." *Chicago Sun-Times* (12 February 1987):82.

Thomas, Mona. "Tony Cragg, morceaux choisis." *Enquêtes et Entretiens* no. 35 (July/September 1988):12.

"Tony Cragg: 'Element Plane.'" *Domus* no. 641 (July/August 1983):67.

Weskott, Hanne. "Tony Cragg: Abfallskulptur des Plastikzeitalters." *Kunstforum International* 49, no. 1 (January 1981):165-66.

Winter, Peter. "Tony Cragg: Puzzlespiel und Superzeichen." *Kunstforum International* 62 (June 1983):56-65.

Winter, Simon Vaughn. "Gary Wragg at ACME, Tony Cragg at Lisson, Trevor Jones at the New Art Centre." *Artscribe* no. 17 (April 1979):52-53.

Zellweger, H. "Englische Plastik Heute." *Kunstwerk* 35 (October 1982):30-31.

STAFF

ADMINISTRATION
Karen Ables, *Accountant*
Christopher Cyga, *Accounting Assistant*
Ursula R. Cyga, *Admissions and Membership Officer*
Carol Lincoln, *Chief Accountant*
Andy Meginnis, *Systems Administrator*
Claire Pardue, *Executive Secretary*
Sandra Peña, *Admissions Assistant*
Jane Piasecki, *Associate Director*
Carolyn Sellers, *Receptionist*

DEVELOPMENT
Kathleen D. Costello, *Associate Director of Development*
Maxine Gaiber, *Public Relations Officer*
Dee Lynn, *Development and Public Relations Assistant*
Margaret O'Malley, *Membership Coordinator*
Charles P. Ries, *Capital Campaign Director*
Aubrey Robin, *Development Clerk*
Margie M. Shackelford, *Director of Development*

EDUCATION
Ellen Breitman, *Director of Education*
Kathy McFarlane, *Education Assistant*
Karin Schnell, *Assistant Director of Education*

EXHIBITIONS
Lucinda Barnes, *Associate Curator*
Paula Chavez, *Registration Intern*
Lorraine Dukes, *Assistant to the Chief Curator*
Marilu Knode, *Assistant Curator*
Betsy Severance, *Registrar*

MUSEUM STORE
Patricia Caspary, *Store Manager*
Henri Lui, *Store Assistant*

OPERATIONS
Chris Gallup, *Preparator*
Dan Goodsell, *Preparator*
Brian Gray, *Exhibition Designer*
Joe Husovsky, *Preparator*
Lynn Kubasek, *Preparator*
Matt Leslie, *Chief of Security*
Richard Tellinghuisen, *Director of Operations*
Robert G. Zingg, *Preparator*

PUBLICATIONS
Sue Henger, *Museum Editor*
Peter Kosenko, *Assistant Editor*
Sandy O'Mara, *Graphic Designer*

SCULPTURE GARDEN CAFE
Marilyn Kaun, *Cafe Manager*

PHOTO CREDITS

Jon and Anne Abbott, courtesy Marian Goodman
    Gallery, New York: 143
Roland Aellig, Bern: 83
Courtesy Galerie Buchmann, Basel: 101, 132
Courtery Galerie Crousel-Robelin Bama, Paris: 39
Courtesy Marian Goodman Gallery: 125, 128,
    129, 130, 148
Hans Gross, courtesy Galerie Buchmann: 93, 116
Tom Haartsen, Amstel: 103
Antxón Hernández, courtesy Galeria Marga Paz,
    Madrid: 133
Bill Jacobson Studio, New York: 115
Andreas Jung, Düsseldorf: 149, 154
Kleinefenn, Paris; courtesy Galerie Crousel-
    Robelin Bama, Paris: 79, 137
Raimund Kummer: 45
Nanda Lanfranco, Genoa: 56
Courtesy Lisson Gallery, London: 113
Heidrun Lohr, Sydney: 158
David Lubarsky, New York: 155
Victor E. Nieuwenhuijs, Amsterdam: 110, 111
Gene Ogami: 87
Susan Ormerod, courtesy Lisson Gallery,
    London: 113
Enzo Ricci, Turin: 93, 146, 156, 157
Gérard Rondeau: 139, 140
Friedrich Rosenstiel, Köln: 99
Jörg Sasse, Düsseldorf: 105, 117, 119, 131, 147
Bent Weber, Hamburg: 145
Gareth Winters, courtesy Lisson Gallery,
    London: cover, 122-23
Courtesy Donald Young Gallery, Chicago: 73,
    150

All other photos courtesy Tony Cragg,
    Wuppertal